MENANDER : SAMIA

MENANDER

SAMIA

edited with translation and notes by

D.M. BAIN

British Library Cataloguing in Publication Data

Menander, *fl. 325-290 B.C.*
  Samia.
  I. Title   II. Bain, D.M.
  882' .01 PA4245.S/

ISBN 0 85668 224 1
ISBN 0 85668 225 X *limp*

Printed and Published by ARIS & PHILLIPS LTD, Warminster, Wilts, England.

CONTENTS

PREFACE

This work is intended to serve as a suitable vehicle for introducing Menander to undergraduates and to scholars who are not specialists in the field of New Comedy. It is hoped that it will encourage them to proceed further and consult more extensive and more learned works. The notes accordingly are for the most part of a very elementary nature. Little in the way of original scholarship will be found in them and references to secondary literature are severely curtailed. I have, however, shown less restraint with regard to the most recent contributions dealing with the text and interpretation of *Samia*.

I started with the intention of producing a translation that would consistently represent modern colloquial English idiom and suppress or entirely recast Greek elements alien to that idiom (e.g. oaths in the name of members of the Greek pantheon, vocative expressions like 'Master' redolent now only of faithful retainers in horror films, and some abusive expressions which have no direct equivalent in English). I found, however, that certain passages defeated my intention and also that there were occasions when, since my translation was designed primarily to help the reader follow the Greek, something closer to the original was demanded. Occasionally archaic English renders Menandrean exploitation of tragic diction: obviosly this is scarcely possible in modern stage dialogue, but I do not know how a translator attempting a version for stage performance is to get round the problem.

Throughout I have been conscious of and tried to give due credit to the work of those scholars who have so enormously advanced the study of Menander in this century. Like the parasite of New Comedy I have taken massive portions from their tables. With regard to *Samia* in particular I must mention here the contributions of Colin Austin and F.H. Sandbach whose annotations have provided the basis for interpretation. The arrangement of my text follows, with some modifications, the format of Sandbach's Oxford Classical Text. I have tried to incorporate in my text or apparatus any information that has come to light since the publication of that edition.

Mr. P.G.McC. Brown was kind enough to glance at a typescript version of my work and his comments have saved me from several errors and misstatements. I am responsible for all errors and omissions that remain. It is a pleasure to thank my publisher for the speed and courtesy with which this book has been seen to production.

David Bain
August 1983

ABBREVIATIONS

(Dates unless there is indication to the contrary are all B.C. It should be noted that I use an extremely Grecizing mode of transliterating Greek. Illogically, upsilon is written as y when it stands on its own, as u when it is part of a diphthong. In the text the numbers in brackets refer to the numeration of *Samia* in Körte's 1938 Leipzig Teubner. Jacques employs a different numbering from that of Sandbach. For a concordance of editions see Gomme-Sandbach, 750ff.: for other Menander plays the numbering is, where possible, that of Sandbach. Non-Menandrean comic fragments are cited from T. Kock, *Comicorum Atticorum Fragmenta*, Leipzig 1880-88.)

Arnott	*Menander*, edited with an English translation by W.G. Arnott, vol. I *Aspis* to *Epitrepontes*, Cambridge, Mass. and London, 1979.
Austin I	*Menandri Aspis et Samia : Textus (cum apparatu critico) et indices*, Berlin, 1969, edidit C. Austin.
Austin II	*Menandri Aspis et Samia : subsidia interpretationis* comparauit C. Austin, Berlin, 1970.
Bain	D. Bain, *Actors and Audience : a Study of Asides and Related Conventions in Greek Drama*, Oxford, 1977.
BICS	*Bulletin of the Institute of Classical Studies*, London.
Blume	H. -D. Blume, *Menanders Samia : eine Interpretation*, Darmstadt, 1974.
Blundell	J. Blundell, *Menander and the Monologue*. Hypomnemata 59, Göttingen, 1980.
CGFPR	*Comicorum Graecorum Fragmenta in Papyris Reperta* edidit C. Austin, Berlin and New York, 1973.
CQ	*The Classical Quarterly*. (n.s. = new series)
CR	*The Classical Review*. (ditto)
Dover, *GPM*	K.J. Dover, *Greek Popular Morality in the Time of Plato and Aristotle, Oxford, 1974.*
GB	Grazer Beiträge.
Gomme-Sandbach	*Menander, a Commentary* by A.W. Gomme and F.H. Sandbach, Oxford, 1973 (= Sandbach ad loc.).
G & R	*Greece and Rome*. (ss = second series)
GRBS	*Greek, Roman and Byzantine Studies*.
Jacques	*Ménandre, tome 1*[1]*: La Samienne:* Texte établi et traduit par J.-M. Jacques, Paris, 1971.
Kasser-Austin	Ménandre, *La Samienne*, publié par R. Kasser avec la collaboration de Colin Austin, Papyrus Bodmer 25, Bibliotheca Bodmeriana, Cologny-Genève, 1969.
K.-T.	*Menandri quae supersunt. Pars altera. reliquiae apud ueteres scriptores seruatae.* edidit A. Körte. opus postumum retractauit, addenda ad utramque partem adiecit A. Thierfelder, Leipzig[2], 1959.

Lowe	J.C.B. Lowe, 'Notes on Menander' *BICS* 20 (1973) 93ff.
LSJ	H.G. Liddell and R. Scott, *A Greek-English Lexicon*, 9th edition revised by Sir H. Stuart-Jones, Oxford, 1940.
Ménandre	*Entretiens sur l'antiquité classique* publiés par Olivier Reverdin, Tome xvi, *Ménandre*, Vandoeuvres-Genève, 1970.
PCPhS	*Proceedings of the Cambridge Philological Society.*
P.Oxy.	The Oxyrhynchus Papyri.
PSI	*Pubblicazioni della Società italiana per la ricerca dei Papiri greci e latini in Egitto.*
P. Tebtun.	The Tebtunis Papyri.
Sandbach	*Menandri Reliquiae Selectae* recensuit F.H. Sandbach, Oxford, 1972 (reprinted with corrections 1976).
Turner	E.G. Turner, *Greek Papyri : an Introduction*, Oxford[2] (paperback) 1980.
ZPE	*Zeitschrift für Papyrologie und Epigraphik.*

INTRODUCTION

1. THE POET AND THE PLAY

     Menander was an Athenian citizen and professional dramatist who competed for monetary prizes at the dramatic festivals of Athens between the years 325-4[1] and 293-2 B.C., probably dying — tradition for what it is worth has it that he drowned while swimming off Peiraieus — soon after that year. At his death he was aged about fifty-two. His plays, unlike those of Aristophanes and the other poets of the fifth-century B.C. who wrote what later came to be known as Old Comedy, were intended for a wider audience than the people of Athens and it is likely that some of them were performed outside Athens during his lifetime. After his death his plays entered the classical repertory all over the Greek world. We know of around 96 titles (he is alleged to have written 105 plays) and, thanks to papyrus-discoveries (see below, section VI), have acquired enough of his work — but only one complete or virtually complete play — to fill a sizeable Oxford Classical Text.[2]

     Menander's second best preserved play, *Samia* (the woman?/'girl' from Samos),[3] cannot be dated with any security: reference to two living individuals in the fourth act ought to help. Unfortunately it does no more than enable us to say that it is not a very late play. Attempts to date the play by stylistic and technical criteria are quite subjective. A betting man might well be advised to put his money on the wager that the first performance of the play took place during the regency of Demetrios of Phaleron, the period 317-307 B.C.

---

1.   For this year (and not 322-1 B.C.) as Menander's debut, see Arnott, xv n. 1, W.B. Dinsmoor, *The Archons of Athens in the Hellenistic Age*, Cambridge, Mass., 1931, 41.
2.   Edited by Sandbach in 1972. Since then considerable portions of the opening of *Misoumenos* have been published, edited by E.G. Turner, first in 'The Lost Beginning of Menander's *Misoumenos*' *Proceedings of the British Academy* 63 (1977) 315-31 (available separately) and then as P. Oxy. 3368-71. The papyrus published by E.W. Handley, *BICS* 26 (1979) 84ff. may come from Menander's *Leukadia* and there have been other lesser discoveries. K. Gaiser has argued at length that *CGFPR* 244, 289 (b), 247,249 — and much else besides — belong to Menander's *Hydria* (*Abhandlungen der Heidelberger Akademie der Wissenschaften*, 1977 and *ZPE* 47 (1982) 11ff.
3.   The French do not have this problem. They can call the play 'La Samienne'.
4.   See Sandbach in Gomme-Sandbach, pp. 542f. and the notes below on 599ff. and 603. The possibility entertained by Moskhion in 628ff. of going as a mercenary to Karia or Baktria provides no decisive evidence for dating. Baktria was a place that required mercenaries during most of Menander's working life and Karia was a trouble spot (cf. Ter. *Eun.* 126) for all but the first ten years of it (see Gomme-Sandbach. p. 543). The most recent account of events in Karia during Menander's lifetime is that of A Mastrocinque, *La Caria e la Ionia meridionale in Epoca ellenistica,* Roma, 1979, 15-43.

II.   THE PLAY : 'QUESTO GIORNO DI TORMENTI!'

The action of the *Samia* spans one hectic and trying day in the life of two Athenian families who live next door to each other. We learn of the events leading up to this day from a member of one of these families, Moskhion, the adopted son of the wealthy Demeas, who owns one of the stage-houses and lives there with his concubine, the Samian courtesan, Khrysis. Demeas and his neighbour, Nikeratos, who is a poor man, have been abroad for some time and are expected back shortly.[1] During their absence, an unfortunate incident took place engendering the action of our play. Khrysis, a popular visitor to Nikeratos' family, held the festival of the Adōnia in Demeas' house, a celebration to which naturally enough Nikeratos' wife and daughter, Plangon, were invited. It chanced that Moskhion came back from Demeas' rural estate on the night of the festival and became an observer of the festivities. This led to an uncharacteristic act. In the heat of the moment he raped Plangon who had wandered off on her own. The girl became pregnant. Moskhion did the right thing, freely confessing his guilt to her mother and promising to marry the girl whenever the two fathers returned. The child, a boy, was accepted by Khrysis who, having had a miscarriage during the period in question, was in a position to pass it off as her own child by Demeas.[2] That this is the intention of Moskhion and his associates becomes clear from the first scene of the play when Parmenon, Demeas' slave, returns from harbour with the news that Demeas and Nikeratos are back. Khrysis, Parmenon and Moskhion go over their plan once more. The immediate problem for Moskhion is to convince Demeas that it is a good idea for him to marry Plangon, to clear Khrysis of any blame for having taken it upon herself to rear her illegitimate child and to make sure that Demeas keeps the child. As it turns out, Moskhion's first task is rendered redundant. During their sojourn abroad the two old men have agreed that it would be an excellent thing if such a marriage took place (what has led them to this we do not know — see the note on 114).

Moskhion succeeds in achieving what he wanted when he meets his father. He manages to persuade Demeas who was greatly disconcerted to find an unexpected and unwelcome child in his house and was intending to throw it and Khrysis out, to change his mind and accept the child. His instant and ready agreement to the proposed marriage may have helped him to win his point. Wedding preparations are set in motion with Parmenon and Nikeratos leaving for market to acquire the necessary provisions and, in the case of Parmenon, to hire a cook. Moskhion also departs thinking it inappropriate to be present while the preparations are made. Demeas gives assistance to his slaves as they get things ready in his house. While he is engaged in this, the crisis of the play arrives and the goal for which both parties are working, the marriage between Moskhion and Plangon, begins to appear unattainable. By accident Demeas happens to overhear the unguarded remarks of an old woman who was once Moskhion's nurse. While talking to the baby she refers to it as Moskhion's. Her behaviour and that of some of the slaves after she has been told that Demeas is within earshot confirm to Demeas that he has overheard a secret. Further confirmation of his worst suspicions comes as he moves to leave his house. He sees Khrysis nursing the baby. Now he believes he has been cuckolded by Moskhion. An encounter with Parmenon, returned from market with the hired cook, brings further corroboration since Parmenon when interrogated confesses in such a way as to confirm Demeas' mistaken impression (see the note on 313ff.). Suppressing his anger, Demeas decides that the best thing to do is to let the wedding continue. He reasons that, if Moskhion was so ready to accept marriage with

xiii

Plangon when it was suggested to him, he wants to escape from Khrysis of whose charms he must have been the unwilling victim. Khrysis (and her baby) will now be shown the door. An uncomprehending Khrysis is driven by Demeas from his house. His desire that the secret of the origin of the child shall not out (and, a little later, the recognition that there is an unwanted observer, the cook) prevents Demeas from spelling out in unambiguous terms the true reason for her ejection. When Demeas returns to the wedding preparations, Nikeratos comes back from market and finds Khrysis, baby in her arms, weeping in front of his front door. He takes her into his house and is unable to comprehend Demeas' volte-face.

The fourth act of the play resolves the problems of the previous three and sees the truth emerge, but only after much discomfort for the principals and indeed a physical confrontation between the two old men. Moskhion returns, impatient for the wedding to take place, and encounters Nikeratos who tells him the strange news about Demeas' change of mind. When Demeas comes out, Moskhion is pushed forward as Khrysis' advocate. Since neither party is aware what the other knows about the true state of affairs (see the note on 464), there follows an encounter at cross-purposes. Eventually, however, Moskhion succeeds in communicating the truth to Demeas and making it clear that while he (Moskhion) is, as Demeas believes, the father of the baby, the mother is not Khrysis. It is Plangon. His efforts to keep this dark from Nikeratos fail and Nikeratos begins to behave in a violent manner towards Khrysis, his own family and anyone who happens to get in his way (Moskhion prudently departs). He has, like Demeas earlier, received confirmation of the unthinkable when, in coming out of the house, he saw Plangon taking the child to her breast. Khrysis and her baby manage to escape Nikeratos' clutches and, while Demeas grapples with his neighbour, she finds her way back into Demeas' house. Demeas by a process of cajolery and tactful humour manages to calm down Nikeratos and assures him that the intended marriage will indeed take place.

All now seems set fair, but Moskhion, piqued because of his father's suspicions and determined to make Demeas suffer a little for them brings a temporary delay to the wedding ceremony and the happy ending that the revelations of the fourth act entail. He returns determined to make a show of defiance so as to teach his father a lesson and force him to some sort of apology. He will pretend to do as other sons at odds with their parents in New Comedy, threatening to go abroad to earn his living as a mercenary soldier.[3] His pretence soon fails, but not before Demeas has delivered a moving and effective speech of apology and remonstrance. Moskhion does not reply to this speech, but during the ensuing confrontation with Nikeratos announces that he has abandoned his resolve. The arrival of his bride and of the wedding procession brings the play to a traditional conclusion, a torchlight procession and appeals to the spectators for their applause and to the goddess Victory for her support.

---

1.   In what we have of the play there is nothing to indicate why the two of them went to Byzantion and the Pontos. There are places where an explanation might have been given — for example the large lacuna in Moskhion's opening speech after line 29. Possibly they went on some sort of public errand.

2.   Doubt must remain about the restoration of 55ff. (see the note ad loc.). It has often been argued that we should not assume that the lines indicated that Khrysis herself had given birth. See C. Dedoussi in her commentary ad loc. (referred to below p.xxiv n.6) and in *Ménandre*, 162, H. Hofmann, 'A new interpretation of certain aspects in Menander's *Samia*' *Proceedings XIV International Congress of Papyrology*, Oxford, 1975, 167ff. (especially 170), N. Holzberg, *Menander : Untersuchungen zur dramatischen Technik*, Nürnberg, 1974, 33 n. 102, and K. Gaiser, *GB* 5 (1976) 111ff. Those who take this view have to assume that at line 266 Khrysis was not feeding the baby, but taking it to herself to calm it down. This seems a forced interpretation of *didousan titthion* (cf. 540).

3.   Note Xenophon, *Anabasis* 6.4.8 where we learn that many of the ten thousand had joined up after running away from their parents. Clinia in Terence's *Hauton Timorumenos* the original of which is Menandrean is another (short-term) mercenary (Ter. *H.T.* 117 *in Asiam ad regem militatum abiit*).

III. THE PLAY IN ITS GENRE

Menander is generally agreed to have been the greatest exponent of the type of drama that came to be known as New Comedy. Certainly after his lifetime during which his success with the public is said to have been less than he deserved he surpassed all his rivals in critical acclaim and, to judge by the proportion of surviving New Comedy papyri that is his, in popularity with the reading public.[1] In fact he is the only New Comic poet with whom we are at all familiar. Practically all of the papyrus fragments of New Comedy which cannot with certainty be attributed to Menander cannot be attributed with anything like probability to anyone else and there is a strong possibility that many of these may be Menandrean. Plautus for the most part adapted plays by authors other than Menander — he adapted Menander's *Adelphoi a, Dis exapatōn* and *Synaristōsai* and the original of *Aulularia* may be Menandrean[2] — and Terence, although favouring Menandrean originals, put on two plays and one scene based on dramatists other than Menander. It is hard, however, to extract from those Latin plays of non-Menandrean provenance a positive picture of any of these other dramatists, playwrights like Philemon and Diphilos[3] (Apollodoros of Karystos the author of the originals of Terence's *Phormio* and *Hecyra* was obviously an admirer and imitator of Menander). There are in any case many difficulties which arise, whenever such an attempt is made, out of the adaptatory techniques of the Latin dramatists. Profitable and valid generalisations about New Comedy are in fact generalisations about Menander. He represents the genre for us.

It is both correct and incorrect to describe *Samia* as a 'typical' example of New Comedy. It conforms to the structure which regularly obtained in the genre and which is displayed in our one complete play, *Dyskolos*. Each play divides into five *merē*[4] (lit. 'parts') or acts — the division is made in the *Dyskolos* by the four time occurrence of the heading XOPOY which must be indicating some kind of choral interlude. Such interludes allow us to imagine time passing sufficient to cover off-stage action: for example, the entracte between the second and third acts of *Samia* accounts for some of the time Parmenon and Nikeratos have spent in getting to the agora and shopping there. The chorus itself, so prominent in Old Comedy, has disappeared from the action of the play and the only notice taken of it during the play is found when it makes its first appearance to end the first 'act': in *Dyskolos* the arrival of a group of drunken Pan-worshippers is announced by one of the actors and we have other such announcements where the speaker declares his intention of getting out of the way of a group of drunken young men.[5] In *Samia* our papyrus has received damage at the point where such an announcement must have occurred (between 204 and 206) — and in fact the play has lost two of its four XOPOYs — but the five-act structure is clear. On the Mytilene mosaic (see below, p.xxiv) the illustration of the scene in which Khrysis is expelled from Demeas' house is labelled Menander's *Samia, Meros* three.

Thematically too, *Samia* contains much that will be familiar to anyone with a passing acquaintance with the genre, a family comedy, mistakes of identity, misunderstanding between father and son, a rape at a festival before the play as the cause of all the trouble. These elements, together with the individual characteristic types, courtesan, young man in love, meddling cook, over-confident slave, are all amply attested elsewhere.[6]

Nevertheless, just as in tragedy Sophokles' *Oidipous* is a single, unique creation which should not be regarded as a paradigm of the genre tragedy, so *Samia* is a single play within the genre. Its plot and action are not closely parallel to any other plays which are well enough known for us to determine their action. The number of characters is very small and the play displays a remarkable concentration of effect — everything builds up to the action-packed fourth act — perhaps, as has been suggested, a concentration which somewhat upsets the balance of the play.[7] With regard to the small number of characters, however, it should be remembered that although only six characters appear before the audience and speak,[8] others are presented to us indirectly. Nikeratos' wife although visible to us perhaps only in the final procession is rendered a fairly vivid presence by what is said about and to her in the play (cf. 200-1 and the note on 421). Likewise some of the members of Demeas' family 'appear' in the play thanks to the virtuoso monologue that opens the third act. Demeas acts the part of the garrulous old nurse and of some of his serving girls.

Anyone who read *Samia* and *Samia* alone would encounter some of what was typical in New Comedy, some of its basic material. He would miss much else. He would be advised to read other plays to find for example the boastful soldier, the fawning parasite (see the note on 603), the grasping courtesan, the shameless pimp, recognition by tokens, intrigues where slave and young man try to get money out of the young man's father. All these features and types were treated at some time and in Menander we have examples of them being subtly reworked.[9] The material of New Comedy is large and varied, more varied than is sometimes made out, and one has the impression that Menander's handling of it and selection from it are extremely sophisticated.

The traditional tripartite division of comedy into 'Old', 'Middle' and 'New' is misleading on several counts.[10] One objection is that it tends to make someone like Menander an innovator rather than a subtle reworker of traditional material. To categorise an author as a writer of 'New Comedy' might be thought to imply that he has somehow chosen to write a kind of drama different from that of his immediate predecessors, the poets of the so-called 'Middle' comedy. In fact the poet of New Comedy is writing at the end of a tradition. The themes and characters are without exception traceable in what has survived (fragments and titles) of middle comedy — that is to say those plays which were performed after the death of Aristophanes and before the theatrical debut of Menander. The poet of 'New' comedy was in a position both advantageous and demanding. He could rely on his audience's familiarity with the conventions and thematic material he was exploiting. He was at the same time obliged to avoid the obvious before an audience that had seen it all before.[11]

1.   For ancient critics' views of Menander see the testimonia 32-49 in K.-T. Note particularly Ploutarkhos, *Comparison of Aristophanes and Menander* [Moralia] 854(3) (= T 41 K.-T.): 'who would enter a theatre if not to see Menander?'. On the papyri of New Comedy see W.G. Arnott, *Arethusa* 3(1970) 49ff. All the papyri of New Comedy that might not be Menandrean published before 1973 are to be found in *CGFPR*.

2.   See Gomme-Sandbach, 4ff.

3.   Even so Günther Jachmann devoted several pages of his *Plautinisches und Attisches* (Berlin, 1931, 98ff.) to an evaluation of the art of Diphilos.

4.   On the five-act form of New Comedy see Gomme-Sandbach, 19f. and on the term *meros, Ménandre*, 253. S.L. Radt, *ZPE* 42 (1980) 5 n.8 points out that the reference there to the commentary on Eupolis' *Marikas* (*CGFPR* 95.97) should be deleted: there 'the fifth part' = 20%.

5.   cf. Men. *Asp.* 246ff. (where the chorus is actually addressed) and *Pk.* 191ff.

6.   See my notes on 23, 38, 50ff., 105, 194, 285, 290, 349, 399ff., 589f., 603, 726f., 733ff. where attention is drawn to typical elements and characters.

7.   So Sandbach apud Gomme-Sandbach, p. 542: 'the first two acts seem, by contrast [with the third and fourth], to have been lacking in tension'.

8. Plangon does not have a speaking part, but she certainly appears in the final procession. Probably her mother does too.

9. cf. Arnott, pp. xxxii ss.

10. See K.J. Dover, *Fifty Years (and twelve) of Classical Scholarship*, Oxford, 1968, 145. Rudolf Kassel and Colin Austin who are engaged in editing the whole corpus of Greek Comedy intend to ignore this classification and arrange the poets alphabetically. An accessible introduction to the poets of Middle Comedy is afforded by W.G. Arnott's 'From Aristophanes to Menander' *G&R* s.s. 19 (1972) 65ff. R.L. Hunter now provides us with a welcome commentary on one of the poets of Middle Comedy in *Eubulus, the Fragments*, Cambridge 1983. For that poet's place in his genre and a defence of the term 'Middle' comedy see pp. 4ff., 20ff. A stimulating discussion of the development of comedy after Aristophanes is supplied by K.J. Dover, *Aristophanic Comedy*, London, 1972, 221ff.

11. See, along these lines, E.W. Handley, 'The conventions of the comic stage and their exploitation by Menander', *Ménandre*, 3ff.

IV. CHARACTERS AND MORALS

Generally speaking the people who appear on Menander's stage are, to use Aristotle's words, 'neither excessively bad' nor 'excessively good'. Most of them would merit the epithet 'decent'. Smikrines, the *poneros* of the *Aspis* is a conspicuous exception[1] and no doubt since Menander wrote plays which involved pornoboskoi (one appears and speaks at *Kolax*, 120ff.) there were further unsympathetic characters. One extremely grasping hetaira is evoked in a particularly famous fragment[2] (but this is someone else's view of her, not necessarily the playwright's. Might not the lady have had some redeeming features? Imagine judging the character of Thais in Terence's *Eunuchus* only on the say of Parmeno![3]) Smikrines is in what we have of Menander the only unredeemed and unredeemable citizen character.

Samia is par excellence a play about basically 'nice' people. Demeas has great energy, generosity and feeling. He admires and cultivates (for reasons we do not know) his poor and irascible neighbour Nikeratos. When he discovers what he thinks to be his son's treachery, he is prepared to make excuses for him, to sweep the trouble under the carpet and make sure for Moskhion's good that the wedding takes place. He is of course grossly unfair to Khrysis, but one must remember that he is in love with her (81) and feels that she has done him a great wrong. His speech of self-justification, delivered at the end of the play to his petulant adopted son, is effective, sincere and entirely convincing. The tact he displays towards Nikeratos in act four is exemplary. He is not perfect. A quick temper and a tendency to rush into things mar or rather humanise his essentially 'good' makeup.[4] Nikeratos has neither the tact nor the wit of his neighbour and when aroused goes to uncontrollable extremes. He remains, however, an essentially likeable figure, cautious of his own and his family's interests, but sympathetic to Khrysis in her distress. Moskhion is an almost excessively timid and restrained young man whose uncharacteristic moment of folly is his tragedy and our comedy. Khrysis, a courtesan respectable enough to be on good terms with the neighbours, is an altruistic person, ready to incur her lover's animosity to help save a child for whom she expresses maternal concern.

Everyone in the play — as one would expect, given their essential lack of malice — aims for the best. The results, however, are nearly disastrous. This is quintessential New Comedy, where the presiding deities, Tykhe (chance) and Agnoia (Misapprehension — the prologue speaker of Menander's *Perikeiromene*) take control and frustrating the plans of mortals ensure that the truth outs and that all is well. An injustice would have been done if Moskhion's scheme had succeeded. A child would have been deprived of its inheritance, an Athenian citizen would have been brought up as a bastard, a potential case for some budding Isaios would have been set in motion.[5] Fortunately the accidents of the third and fourth acts lead to Demeas learning the truth and, after considerable discomfort for all of the principals, all ends happily.

Before the discovery of the end of the play that came with the publication of the Bodmer Codex (see below, p.xxiii), it has been suggested that Khrysis, whose conduct in the play is faultless, but who suffers more than anyone else, being subjected to totally unjustified suspicion and abuse, might have at the end met with some reward. For example, she might turn out to be an Athenian, a long lost sister of Moskhion and Demeas might take it upon himself to legitimise their union and marry her. Now we know this to be quite false. No one addresses a word of apology to Khrysis once the truth comes out and after she has escaped from Nikeratos and returned to Demeas' house we see her again but once, as a mute participant in the wedding-procession. Are we to view this as a reflection of a limit of interest on the part of the dramatist in the non-citizen character or, perhaps the more likely explanation, a result of Menander being more interested dramatically in the Demeas-Moskhion relationship than in that between Demeas and Khrysis?[6]

Some have found in Menander a dramatist who through the medium of his plays sought to improve the morals of his time and to make criticisms of the society in which he lived. This was a case easier to sustain when all we had of him was fragmentary quotation. The anthology of Stobaios teems with high-flown moral generalities culled from Menander's plays. It was easy from this evidence to infer that Menander was a sententious writer. Now when, as happens from time to time, we are given the opportunity through the discovery of papyri of seeing such quotations in their dramatic context, the picture changes. Often we find noble sentiments placed in the mouths of characters who have no true claim to express them or else brought to bear on a situation where they do not apply. In *Samia* it would be a mistake to regard 140ff. which we already knew from Stobaios as fr. 248 K.-T. as an attempt to educate the Athenian people and make them feel more sympathetic towards the plight of illegitimate children. The person who speaks the lines, Moskhion, is attempting to deceive his father, to persuade him to accept as his own Moskhion's baby. There is also an element of comedy about the situation in which the lines are delivered. These lofty sentiments flow from the mouth of a young man lecturing his father (cf. the scene in Men. *Dysk*, 817 where Kallippides on the receiving end of a long harangue from his son on the topic of wealth legitimately objects 'why do you say gnōmai to me?'). As Aristotle notes (Arist. *Rhetoric* 1395[a]2-7) '*gnōmologein* (talking sententiously) is appropriate to older people and about things of which a person has experience'.

That there is considerable moral subtlety in Menander is not to be denied. Moral points in Menander, however, are unobtrusive, and the moralising pill has often a coating of humorous sugar. The speech of Demeas rebuking his son in the fifth act strikes home even though the son's (delayed) response to it is in the form of a kind of joke.[7] In it generality is avoided and the appropriate points made with clarity and passion. Menander's reputation as a sent7entious author is undeserved.

---

1. Tykhe the prologue deity describes him quite explicitly as 'bad': 'he outdoes everyone in *ponēria*' (Men. *Asp*. 116).

2. fr. 185 K.-T.

3. On the unjust suspicions that are harboured against Thais in *Eunuchus* see W. Steidle, *Rheinisches Museum* 116 (1973) 326ff.

4. It may be that his failure to discharge the normal Athenian obligation of reproducing himself is meant to make us take him less seriously as a person. But since this play demands for its plotting a concubine living with the young man's father, Demeas' bachelorhood is probably determined. We cannot exclude the possibility that he was a widower. The analogy of Terence's *Adelphoi* (= Menander, *Adelphoi* b) suggests that he was not. Moskhion's adoption may have been for the express purpose of finding an heir (although in that case, as Peter Brown puts to me, why adopt at so young an age?).

5. It does not seem likely, although it cannot be excluded, that passing the baby off as Khrysis' was only the first stage of the plan and that Moskhion would later tell the truth about the child. The dramatic tension would be considerably reduced if this was the case. E. Keuls *ZPE* 10 (1973) 18 cannot be correct in believing that at the end of the play Khrysis keeps the baby.

6. cf. E. Fantham, *Phoenix* 29 (1975) 66. It is in any case a 'law' of New Comedy that a girl discovered to be an Athenian should have an intact reputation (note the implications of Men. *Sik*. 370ff.).

7. See the note on 724f.

V. DRAMATIC FORM AND CONVENTIONS

Like all of the drama produced at Athens, Menander's plays are written in verse.[1] By Menander's time the wide metrical variety of Old Comedy had been reduced drastically — the disappearance of the chorus from the action of the play no doubt being largely contributory to this process[2] — and the reader of *Samia* is faced with only two types of line:[3]

(a) The iambic trimeter,[4] the commonest dialogue metre of Greek drama, of which the the strictest form would be

$$x\underline{\overset{2}{}}u\underline{\overset{4}{}} \quad x\underline{\overset{6}{}}u\underline{\overset{8}{}} \quad x\underline{\overset{10}{}}u\underline{\overset{12}{}}$$

(x represents '*syllaba anceps*' $\underline{u}$: the last element of the line may contain a short syllable: '*breuis in longo*'.)

The comic trimeter is considerably freer than the tragic one and resolution of the long elements '*longa*' is frequent (all except the final one may be resolved) as is the treatment of the *syllabae ancipites* as *longa* to be resolved (cf. *anamein-* in line 60), a licence only permitted in tragedy when proper names are involved.

The strict rules regarding caesura which tragedy almost inevitably observes (word-end after the fifth or seventh element) are occasionally breached in comedy and 'Porson's law' which bans word-end of a 'polysyllable' directly after the ninth element if a cretic shaped word concludes what remains of the line is often ignored. There are, however, in New Comedy passages where the rules of tragedy are observed for a significant length of time (e.g. *Sam.*625-29) and these are not just confined to lines which quote tragedy. The effect may be to introduce seriousness and pathos, but it is not easy to gauge.[5] On tragic prosody see 517 note.

(b) The trochaic tetrameter

$$\underline{\overset{1}{}}u\underline{\overset{3}{}}x \quad \underline{\overset{5}{}}u\underline{\overset{7}{}}x \quad \underline{\overset{9}{}}u\underline{\overset{11}{}}x \quad \underline{\overset{13}{}}u\underline{\overset{15}{}}$$

in which there is word-end after the eighth element (*Sam.* 484 is exceptional: see the note there). A certain amount of resolution is possible, but resolution of the fourth element is rare.

The whole of the fourth act of *Samia* is written in this metre. It seems likely that its effect was felt to be more mouvemente than that of the trimeter. It has to be noted, however, that there are passages in New Comedy where, although the metre is the tetrameter, speed is hardly demanded (notably the last act speech of Demeas in this play and the 'apologia pro uita sua' of Knemon at Men. *Dysk.* 708ff.). The final scene of *Samia* (670-730) is also written in this metre. Exceptionally the formulaic ending — an appeal for the audience's applause and a prayer for victory — is included (with the requisite expansion) within the trochaic complex: on other occasions we find a trochaic ending abandoned so that we can return to the iambic formula.

As with most New Comedy, a day encompasses the action of *Samia* and when the play ends we are to imagine that it is evening. Likewise one place suffices for the locale of the play. The set (that is to say the front of the stage-building, the *skene*) represents the front of two neighbouring houses with their doors facing on to an Athenian street (whether there was a third door unused and uncommented upon — other plays like *Dyskolos* require *three* doors — or whether it was blocked over is debatable). In this play one of the side entrances (originally *eishodoi* but by now perhaps *parhodoi*[6]) represents the way to Peiraieus, the other the way to the agora: it is again debatable which (right or left?) represented which.

New Comedy appears to have been played with a company of three actors[7] who shared the parts between them. *Samia* with as far as we know only six speaking parts presents no real difficulties to such a small company, although by the standards of the modern theatre the sharing of roles seems odd, the same actor at one time or another playing both Moskhion and Demeas or Demeas then Khrysis. It must be remembered that the actors, who were all men, wore masks. Obviously considerable vocal expertise and mimetic powers were demanded of the Greek comic actor. In his monologue at the beginning of the third act Demeas plays more than one part within the same speech (cf. above, p.xvi).

By Menander's time we find that comedy has developed a system of conventions regarding entering and awareness on stage, a system that suggests a description of it as a somewhat stylised genre.[8] Various patterns of events relating to the entrance of actors recur. One is the very useful form of entrance where two characters enter continuing a conversation begun off-stage (as at 61ff. in this play). It is also very frequent for an entrant coming from the stage-building to conclude a conversation with the unseen denizens of the house before turning round and discovering that he is not alone (cf. Nikeratos at 421 and Demeas at 440). Characters also enter soliloquizing and then observe that they are not alone: so Nikeratos returning from market at 399 breaks off his soliloquy in surprise when he observes Khrysis.

Eavesdropping[9] is a common device of New Comedy. It is surprisingly common in situations where the eavesdropper does not learn anything of value or has no real motive for self-concealment. Notice how Khrysis retreats and listens in on the conversation of Moskhion and Parmenon (61ff.) when one might have expected that she would immediately approach the two who were to be her allies in the coming intrigue.

The most striking technical feature of *Samia* is its extensive use of monologues: 'when we make allowances for lacunae, monologue can hardly count for less than 370 lines in a play of about 900 [on the length of the play see below, p.xxiv, n.8]'.[10] The two principal characters, Moskhion and Demeas are the main users of this medium of communication (although Nikeratos and Khrysis also deliver monologues). The use of monologue enables the audience (and us) to learn the feelings and reactions of characters which would not have come out in the course of dialogue: for most of this play Demeas and Moskhion have something to conceal from some of the other characters. The very lengthy monologue delivered by Demeas at the beginning of the third act is an actor's tour de force, containing a sequence of changing moods, a vivid narrative made more vivid by the speaker taking on and playing the parts of some of the people he is describing.

Monologues contain a great deal of material that might be described as 'audience-address' and indeed there are places within them where it is made quite clear that the speaker is talking directly to the audience.[11] This is a legacy of Old Comedy.[12] New Comedy is continuing a tradition, but achieving or intending an effect more subtle than the one found in that genre. Our actors no longer harangue the audience and make jokes about or involving them: they confide in them. One is probably entitled to speak of Demeas in this play having a special rapport with the audience.[13]

1. A tiny fraction of Old Comedy — mostly parody of sacral or official language — is prose. See R. Kassel, *Dichtkunst und Versifikation bei den Griechen, Rheinisch-Westfälische Akademie der Wissenschaften, Geisteswissenschaften Vorträge* G 250 (1981)21.
2. On lyric in post-Aristophanic comedy see R.L. Hunter, *ZPE* 36(1979)33ff.
3. Menander's *Dyskolos* presented us with a metre that one might have imagined would have disappeared from comedy, the iambic tetrameter catalectic. His *Leukadia* (influence of Euripides' *Iphigeneia in Aulis*?) opened with anapaests. The hexameter song which may come from *Theophoroumene* (see E.W. Handley, *BICS* 16(1969)95ff.) would be a song sung by a character who is possessed and therefore constitutes a special case.

4.   The fullest account of this and of the trochaic tetrameter in Menander is to be found in the introduction of E.W. Handley's edition of *Dyskolos* (London, 1965), pp. 56ff. See also Gomme-Sandbach, pp. 36ff. for a discussion which, although brief, is much more exhaustive than the one given here.

5.   The same goes for the use of tragic diction. See Sandbach, *Ménandre*, 126f.

6.   For these terms see O. Taplin, *The stagecraft of Aeschylus*, Oxford, 1977, 449ff.

7.   See Gomme-Sandbach, pp. 16ff. and Sandbach in *Le Monde Grec* (Hommages à Claire Préaux) Brussels, 1975, 197ff.

8.   On the degree of conventionality of New Comedy see Bain, 148ff., where it is pointed out that Menander is much more realistic or much less conventional than the poets of Roman Comedy in dispensing with or being very sparing with the use of 'stage-directional phrases'.

9.   See Bain, 105ff.

10.   Blundell, 44. He gives an excellent account of the monologues of the last three acts, 35ff.

11.   cf. 5, 33, 269, 447, 683.

12.   See Bain, 98 n.2. Tragedy does not admit this kind of effect: see Bain, *CQ* n.s. 25(1975)13ff.

13.   cf. Bain, 206f. and Blundell, 41f.

VI.   THE TEXT – THE RECOVERY OF MENANDER[1]

It is only by happy accident that we possess as much as we have of *Samia*, considering that Menander, as an author of whom we had first-hand knowledge, disappeared from human ken for thirteen centuries. Menander's survival is of a kind quite different from that of Aristophanes, his peer in the older genre. Eleven plays by the latter have been preserved for us because they continued to be read and copied at Byzantion during the middle ages. Menander's plays did not achieve this treatment – they did not succeed in becoming Byzantine school books[2] – and until the end of last century our knowledge of him depended (with the exception of one very early parchment codex) entirely on quotations in other authors and on the filter of Latin adaptation (cf. above, p.xv). Fortunately excavation in Egypt brought about a revival of his fortunes. The capacity of the papyrus plant to provide a material for book production that would survive in dry conditions led in the last ninety or so years to the recovery of a mass of lost Greek literature including lost works and parts of works by authors already fairly well-known and more strikingly the recovery of lost (or virtually lost) authors like Bakkhylides, Herodas and – Menander.[3]

Our knowledge of *Samia* depends for the most part on the recovery of two papyrus books, one discovered in the first decade of our century, the other some time in the fifties. These are the C and B of the apparatus.

C is a papyrus book written in the IV-V centuries A.D. It belonged to a lawyer named Flavius Dioscurus who lived during the sixth century A.D. at the village of Kome Aphrodite (Aphrodito – the modern Kom Ishqaw) on the upper Nile. The book had been dismantled and used to wrap up documents which were kept in a jar. It is now kept in the Egyptian museum in Cairo (hence 'C') and recently an excellent photographic edition of it has been published by the London Institute of Classical Studies.[4]

C, while preserving no one play in its entirety, contains considerable portions of three plays, *Epitrepontes*, *Perikeiromene* and a play it was guessed was entitled *Samia*–later discoveries, the Mytilene mosaic and the Bodmer codex have confirmed this guess which some had not accepted[5] – in fact lines 216-416 and 547-581 of our play. C also includes some smaller items, including the opening scene of *Heros*. Several editions of Menander based upon C have appeared. Alfred Körte's 1938 Teubner became the standard edition.[6]

B is P. Bodmer XXV, an acquisition of the Swiss collector, Martin Bodmer. About its discovery and provenance nothing authenticated has been revealed.[7] The book[8] which was written in the third century A.D. contained three plays, *Samia, Dyskolos* and *Aspis*.[9] The almost complete *Dyskolos* was first published in 1957, but publication of the other two plays had to wait till 1969, the delay arising from the hope, barely fulfilled, that more of the book would come to light.

B. contains of *Samia* lines 1-245. 254-406. 411-454, 458-605, 612-737. Since 254-416 and 612-86 are preserved in both B and C we are for these lines placed in the unusual position of having variants to choose from in a Menander text.

Two further papyri of *Samia* have since appeared:
- (a)   P. Oxy. 2831 (0 16 Sandbach) – 2nd to 3rd cent. A.D.[10] – contains the ends of lines 385-90 and actually provides us with a third witness for the text of these lines.
- (b)   P. Oxy. 2943 (0 17 Sandbach, *CGFPR* 183), second century A.D., [11] containing the ends of 120-5 (missing in B) and the beginnings of 134-42.

Only four 'book' fragments of *Samia* are known, one of which, the fragment printed at the end of the text, may be misattributed (see the note ad loc.). The other two, frr. 248, 249 K.-T. coincide respectively with lines 140-2 and 163-4. Neither is attributed by their source, Stobaios, to *Samia*. The first is cited from *Knēdia*, the second from *Kēdeia* or *Akēdeia*. Clearly *Samia* was one of those Menander plays which had a double title[12] (like *Dyskolos/Misanthropos, Misoumenos/ Thrasonides*). The title suggested by the MSS of Stobaios is *Kēdeia*, the abstract noun meaning 'connection by marriage' which is very apt, considering the plot of the play. Other interpretations fail to convince.[13] Finally, Favorinos in his *peri phygēs* uses, without naming the play, part of line 209 (= Menander, fr. 701 K.-T.).

It can be seen, then, that the play received comparatively little attention in antiquity.[14] Outside literature, however, we have further testimony. One of the Menandrean scenes depicted in the famous house of mosaics in Mytilene (dated to the fourth century A.D.)[15] is the ejection of Khrysis that took place in the third act of our play. The scene is headed '*Menandrou Samia, meros gamma*' and the three participants, Demeas, Khrysis and the cook are named. At the time this discovery settled once and for all dispute over the title of the play and removed doubts whether the cook was present during this scene.

1. There are several excellent accounts available for the reader wishing more detail and documentation on this topic, e.g. Arnott, xxvi-xxx, Gomme-Sandbach, 3f. and W.G. Arnott, *Arethusa* 3 (1970) 49ff. (for discoveries since the *Dyskolos*).
2. Menander's future as a school author was impeded by his language. The Attic he wrote met with censure from grammarians who insisted on a return to the 'pure' Attic of Aristophanes and some of the orators. See, for a succinct introduction to the phenomenon known as 'Atticism', R. Browning, *Medieval and Modern Greek*, London, 1969, 49ff. (cf. also L.D. Reynolds and N.G. Wilson, *Scribes and Scholars*, Oxford[2] 1974, 39ff.). Some grammarians tolerated Menander. See K. Alpers, *Das attizistische Lexikon des Oros (Sammlung griechischer und lateinischer Grammatiker[4]*), Berlin, 1981.67.
3. For an account of the literature we have recovered from the papyri see Turner, 97ff. For the most recent discoveries see P.J. Parsons, 'Facts from Fragments', *G&R* s.s. 29 (1982) 184ff.
4. *The Cairo Codex of Menander (P. Cair, J. 43227)* London, 1978: Plates xxxvii-xlvi contain the *Samia*.
5. For an illuminating account of what scholars made of the *Samia* as transmitted in the Cairo codex and of the occasions where they went wrong (as well as an attractive introduction to the interpretation of the play itself) see Hugh Lloyd-Jones, 'Menander's Samia in the Light of the New Evidence', *Yale Classical Studies* 22 (1972) 119ff.
6. There is an excellent commentary on the Cairo *Samia* written (in demotic Greek) by C. Dedoussi, Athens, 1965. For new readings derived from the photographs and re-examination relating to *Samia* see H. Riad, *ZPE* 11(1973) 204ff., F.H. Sandbach, *ZPE* 40 (1980) 51 and Koenen's introduction to the photographic edition.
7. See Turner, 201f.
8. One scrap, P. Barc(inonensis) 45, somehow found its way to Barcelona: R. Kasser provides a very full account of the makeup and arrangement of B in Kasser-Austin, 7ff. Lowe, 94f. calculates the length of the play at about 895 lines. P.Barc.45 contains parts of lines 399-410, 446-457 (the editio princeps by R. Roca-Puig, *Boletin de la Real Academia de Buenas Letras de Barcelona* 32 (1967-8)ff. contains a photograph of P. Barc.).
9. For discussion of the possibility that Menander's work appeared at one time in triads, see A. Blanchard, *Proceedings of the sixteenth international congress of papyrology*, Ann Arbor, 1981, 24ff.
10. First published by E.G. Turner in *Aegyptus* 47 (1967 - appeared 1970) 186ff.
11. First published in 1972 but already made public in *CR* n.s. 21 (1971) 352ff. = *CGFPR* 183.
12. See K. Gaiser, *Menander, Der Schild oder die Erbtochter*, Zürich, 1971, 21n.5 and R.L. Hunter, *Eubulus, the Fragments* (Cambridge, 1983), 146-7.
13. e.g. those of N. Holzberg, *Menander; Untersuchungen zur dramatischen Technik*, Nürnberg, 1974, 33 n.102, Q. Cataudella, *GB* 2 (1974) 15ff., K. Gaiser, *GB* 5 (1976) 99ff. The earlier discussions by H.-J. Mette, *Lustrum* 13 (1968) 547 and *Hermes* 97 (1969) 435 in which it was suggested that 'Akedeia' was the name of the prologue deity cannot stand in the light of the Bodmer codex.
14. There may be reference to this play in the sixth-century A.D. rhetor Khorikios. 32, 73 Foerster-Richtig 'Moskhion has taught us to rape girls', but Moskhion is a common name for the young man in Comedy.
15. See S. Charitonidis, L. Kahil, R. Ginouvès, *Les Mosaïques de la Maison du Ménandre à Mytilène (Antike Kunst Beiheft* 6, 1970). The *Samia* scene is also reproduced in *Ménandre* as plate IA between pp.246-47 and in Kasser-Austin, 6.

It was said in the previous section that the Bodmer papyrus 'contained' lines 1-245 etc. This was an exaggeration. A glance at the first page (Kasser-Austin contains photographs 're-duced by a little over a quarter' of all of the *Samia*) shows that a good many of the lines are defective in one way or another. There are gaps in the papyrus, sometimes at the beginning of the lines, sometimes at the end and sometimes in the middle. In some places the ink has faded or been scraped away so that some letters can no longer be read. The editor of a papyrus text is constantly confronted by problems that only irregularly confront the editor of a text with a manuscript tradition and the special circumstances of transmission necessitate a special mode of presentation.[1] The editor, depending on what sort of edition he wishes to produce, has a certain latitude with regard to how much he communicates to the reader about the physical appearance of the papyrus. He is obliged to indicate where the text is seriously defective, but if he is pro-ducing a text for the general reader he does not want to trouble him with trivia in those passages where the text, although incomplete, can be restored with certainty. Readers are warned that in the text printed below[2] I go even less far than Sandbach (see pp. v ss.) in attempting to give an. idea of the makeup of the original papyri; for that sort of information the reader must go to the photographs and transcript of Kasser-Austin, to Austin I and II 104ff. and to the recent photo-graphic reproduction of the Cairo codex. Even so I adopt some papyrological conventions which the reader unfamiliar with papyrus texts may not have encountered. A brief description of them follows.

In order to indicate a gap in the papyrus the editor uses square brackets. The fragmentary line in *Samia* which is numbered 2 has neither beginning nor end. We print it thus:

$\quad\quad$] . νε˙ τί λυπῆσαί με δεί [

(the dot before the nu indicates a letter or space for a letter which cannot be read). For a gap within a line of which the beginning and end are preserved we use an open bracket then a closed one.

When the left hand margin of a column of text is tolerably well preserved we are often in a position to calculate the number of letters missing in lines where there are gaps. For example, on the basis of lines 198ff. where the margin is intact, one can be fairly certain of the number of letters missing in the two preceding lines and restore accordingly. When we have calculated the number of letters missing in a line, but decided that the original reading is irrecoverable, we print the line with the appropriate number of dots within the bracketed space. For example, line 454 is printed thus:

$\quad\quad$ . . . . . .] πρεσβεύεταί τις πρός με ˙δεινόν. - οὐχί σόν

(where it is reckoned that six letters are missing at the start of the line). There are a good many passages where, although the papyrus is defective,because of the satisfactory nature of the sur-rounding context we are in a position to say with near certainty what the missing part must have contained. Obviously this is the case when only one letter is missing. In line 26 there can be no doubt that Menander wrote ὑπ' ἀντεραστῶν even though we do not have the pi that was the second letter of the line. Normally such restored or supplemented letters are printed within square brackets (in this text I follow Sandbach in not troubling the reader when I judge there to be no doubt about the restoration). Supplementation is rarely as easy as this and editors now show a great deal more restraint in filling in the gaps than was shown in the early days of papyrology. The confidence of earlier editors has often been shown to have been mistaken by new discoveries. In this play we now have the Bodmer papyrus to set beside the Cairo codex. It often exposes earlier mistaken supplementation of C.[3] The text I print is a little more heavily restored than Sandbach's: some restorations are printed exempli gratia.

Editors use another type of bracket. When the editor wishes to indicate to the reader that he is restoring something which has been accidentally omitted from the papyrus, he uses angular brackets, Line 445 is defective metrically — it is a syllable short — and syntactically. The writer of the papyrus omitted οὕς. His mistake arose because, once he had written these letters as the end of the preceding word, he imagined he had already written the omitted word (the error is known as haplography). Accordingly we print the line thus:

$$\dot{ε}π' \ \dot{α}γαθῆι \ τύχηι \ τε \ π\tilde{α}σι \ τοὺς \ γάμους \ < οὕς > \ μέλλομεν.$$

Another papyrological practice should be mentioned here if only to warn the reader that it is not adopted in this edition. It often happens that the papyrus preserves only a *part* of a letter, a 'trace'. In such instances if one chooses to print a letter it is customary to put a dot under it. There is an unfortunate ambiguity about the use of this sign since no distinction is made between a thoroughly damaged letter whose identity is the editor's guess (it may still be a certain restoration) and a slightly damaged letter which is palaeographically quite certain.[4]

The reader should be warned that what is printed under the text (the 'apparatus criticus') is highly selective, indicating only those places where (what seems to the author) a serious or interesting textual question arises and making little attempt to render a consistent account of the appearance of the papyri that preserve our play (occasionally information that has come to light since the publication of Sandbach's text is recorded even though the textual 'interest' of such additions might not be regarded as particularly significant). An idiosyncrasy of the apparatus is that no names of modern scholars appear in it, only the symbols indicating the four papyri, the names z of the ancient authors who quote from the play and the symbol z[5] which denotes a change in the transmitted text made by some modern scholar or scholars. I do not indicate who is responsible for supplements adopted in the text. This information is available in the editions. Where some new suggestion is adopted I have attempted in the commentary to apportion the credit where it is due.

1.   See Turner, 54ff.
2.   Some very fragmentary lines (142b-1 Sandbach and 167-88 Sandbach) have been omitted altogether.
3.   e.g. line 330 (= 115 in the Cairo codex) was restored thus:

$$εἰ \ μὲν \ γὰρ \ \mathring{η} \ βουλόμενος \ \mathring{η} \ δουλούμενος.$$

δουλούμενος became the vulgate. No one suggested the reading of the Bodmer codex, κεκνισμένος.
4.   See Turner, 70f.
5.   In this I follow the practice adopted by K.J. Dover in his Theocritus, *Select Poems*, London, 1971.

VIII. ATTRIBUTION AND IDENTIFICATION OF SPEAKERS

The various means used in antiquity to indicate the identity of speakers in dramatic texts[1] might be thought to show the same absence of consideration for the ancient reader as is displayed by the lack of word-division or of thoroughgoing punctuation in the texts. The modern practices of placing the name of the character (or an abbreviation of the name) beside what he had to say and of indicating exits and entrances by means of stage directions[2] were never developed in antiquity. Names appear sporadically in the margins and between the lines in our texts, particularly on the first entrance of a character, but these were put there by the reader, not the playwright in order to ease his own task. The full name on entrance as in 62f. will be an editorial addition

Change of speaker was indicated by various symbolic systems. The one used in the two papyri which are our main witnesses for *Samia* (and which seems characteristic of books in the late empire) employs two symbols. The first of these is the horizontal line under the left margin of the text, the *paragraphos*. The other is the double dot, *dikōlon*, placed within or at the end of a line. In B and C these two symbols are used in conjunction. The paragraphos under a line indicates a change of speaker within or at the end of that line.[3] The *dikōlon* marks where one character's utterance terminates. The dialogue between Parmenon and Moskhion at 62f. in B looks like this;

ΠΑΡΜΕΝΩΝ (This is his entrance)

οὔκουν ἀκούεις; φημί : καὶ τὸν γείτονα

(The first line contains one change of speaker; Moskhion takes over from Parmenon after the *dikōlon*) and then

πάρεισιν : εὖ γ' ἐπόησαν : ἀλλ' ὅπως ἔσει . . .

(Here there are two changes of speaker. Parmenon answers. Then Moskhion continues until the second *dikōlon* when Parmenon begins to speak again.)

It would be no service to the reader to reproduce this system and I follow the method of modern editors in inserting abbreviations of the character's names at appropriate points. When the name is found on the papyrus it is left unbracketed. When there is no attestation of a name, but there are *paragraphoi* and *dikōla* indicating change of speaker, the name is inserted within round brackets. When, however, a modern scholar's suggestion is adopted and a change from the attribution implied by a papyrus accepted, the abbreviated name will have angular brackets round it.

---

1. J.C.B. Lowe's article in *BICS* 9 (1962) 27ff. remains the standard study of this topic. We have acquired more evidence from the papyri since he wrote (N.B. the use in a Vienna papyrus of Aristophanes' *Peace* of a *paragraphos* to indicate stage-business: see A. Carlini, *Papiri letterari greci*, Pisa, 1978, p.138).

2. Greek dramatists did not write their own stage directions. Instead they composed their dialogue in such a way that the movements on stage could be inferred from what the actors said (see O. Taplin, 'Did Greek Dramatists write stage instructions?' *PCPhS* n.s. 23 (1977) 121ff.). Such stage directions as appear in Menandrean papyri are readers' additions (see Bain, 132f.).

3. The *dikōlon* is used also to indicate not a change of speaker, but a change of addressee (e.g. in C (but not in B) in line 614 a dikolon follows *well done!* which is addressed to Nikeratos, what follows being soliloquy).

FURTHER READING

This list is confined to items not mentioned in the abbreviations, introduction or notes.

W.S. Anderson, 'The Ending of the *Samia* and other Menandrian Comedies', *Studi classici in onore di Quintino Cataudella* II, Catania, 1972, 155ff.

W.G. Arnott, *Menander, Plautus, Terence* (*Greece and Rome*, new surveys in the classics, 9), Oxford, 1975.

———— , 'Time, Plot and Character in Menander', *ARCA* (*Papers of the Liverpool Latin Seminar*) 2 (1979) 343ff.

———— , 'Moral Values in Menander', *Philologus* 125 (1981) 215ff.

L. Casson, *The Plays of Menander*, New York, 1971 (contains a prose translation of *Samia*).

S. Goldberg, *The Making of Menander's Comedy*, London, 1980.

E.W. Handley, chapters on Menander and New Comedy in *The Cambridge History of Classical Literature* I, Cambridge, 1983.

A.G. Katsouris, *Linguistic and Stylistic Characterization : Tragedy and Menander*, Ioannina, 1974.

———— , *Tragic Patterns in Menander*, Athens, 1975.

P.-E. Legrand, *Daos : Tableau de la Comédie grecque pendant la période dite nouvelle*, Lyon, 1910.

F.H. Sandbach, *The Comic Theatre of Greece and Rome*, London, 1977.

S. Trenkner, *The Greek Novella in the Classical Period*, Cambridge, 1958.

E.G. Turner, *The Girl from Samos or The In-Laws*, London, 1972 (verse translation designed for a radio production and consequently very freely restored).

———— , 'Menander and the New Society of his Time', *Chronique d'Égypte* 54 (1979) 106ff.

———— , 'The Rhetoric of Question and Answer in Menander', *Themes in Drama 2*, Cambridge, 1980, 1ff.

T.B.L. Webster, *Menander, an Introduction*, Manchester, 1974.

U. von Wilamowitz-Moellendorff, *Menander : Schiedsgericht*, Berlin, 1925 (contains in pp. 119ff. a characteristically brilliant and stimulating introduction to New Comedy).

ΣΑΜΙΑ

Η

ΚΗΔΕΙΑ

THE SAMIAN GIRL

OR

THE MARRIAGE TIE

SIGLA (v. etiam pp.xxiii s.)

B	P. Bodmer 25 (P. Barcinonensi 45 inclusa)
C	P. Cairensis 43227
O^1	P. Oxyrhynchica 2831
O^2	P. Oxyrhynchica 2943
z	coniectura alicuius uiri docti
[B]	lectio libri B propter lacunam ignoratur
[[α]]	littera a librario deleta
om.	omisit
Stob.Ecl.	Stobaeus, *Eclogae*.

TA TOY ΔΡΑΜΑΤΟΣ ΠΡΟΣΩΠΑ

ΜΟΣΧΙΩΝ   υἱὸς ποιητὸς Δημέου
ΧΡΥΣΙΣ   ἑταίρα Σαμία, παλλακὴ Δημέου
ΠΑΡΜΕΝΩΝ   θεράπων Δημέου
ΔΗΜΕΑΣ   γέρων Ἀθηναῖος
ΝΙΚΗΡΑΤΟΣ γέρων Ἀθηναῖος, γείτων Δημέου, πατὴρ
           Πλαγγόνος
ΜΑΓΕΙΡΟΣ

ΚΩΦΑ ΠΡΟΣΩΠΑ
   ΘΕΡΑΠΟΝΤΕΣ ΔΗΜΕΟΥ
   ΑΚΟΛΟΥΘΟΙ ΤΟΥ ΜΑΓΕΙΡΟΥ
   ΠΛΑΓΓΩΝ θυγατὴρ Νικηράτου
   ΛΟΥΤΡΟΦΟΡΟΣ
   ΟΙΚΕΤΑΙ ΔΗΜΕΟΥ ΚΑΙ ΝΙΚΗΡΑΤΟΥ
   ? ΤΡΥΦΗ, θεράπαινα Δημέου

CHARACTERS OF THE PLAY

MOSKHIŌN   *adopted son of Demeas*
KHRŸSIS   *courtesan from Samos, Demeas' concubine*
PARMENŌN *one of Demeas' slaves*
DĒMEĀS   *an elderly Athenian gentleman*
NĪKĒRATOS *an elderly Athenian, neighbour to Demeas*
                 and father of Plangon
A COOK

SILENT CHARACTERS

    ATTENDANTS OF DEMEAS
    THE COOK'S RETINUE
    PLANGŌN, *Nikeratos' daughter*
    THE WATER CARRIER
    MEMBERS OF THE HOUSEHOLDS OF DEMEAS AND
      NIKERATOS
    ? TRYPHĒ, *Demeas' slave*

ΜΕΡΟΣ Α

[ΜΟΣΧΙΩΝ]

                              ]περ[
         ].νε˙ τί λυπῆσαί με δεῖ [
......όδ]υνηρόν ἐστιν˙ ἡμάρτηκα γάρ.
......]ο τοῦτο ἐσόμενον λογίζομαι,
μᾶλλον] δὲ τοῦτ' ἂν εὐλόγως ὑμῖν ποεῖν   5
ἅπαντα] τὸν ἐκείνου διεξελθὼν τρόπον.
οἷς μὲ]ν ἐτρύφησα τῶι τότ' εὐθέως χρόνωι
ὢν παι]δίον, μεμνημένος σαφῶς ἐῶ˙
εὐεργέ]τει γὰρ ταῦτά μ'οὐ φρονοῦντά πω.
ὡς δ' ἐν]εγράφην οὐδὲν διαφέρων οὐδενός,   10
τὸ λεγόμενον δὴ τοῦτο "τῶν πολλῶν τις ὤν",
πέφυκ]α μέντοι, νὴ Δί', ἀθλιώτερος –
αὐτοὶ] γάρ ἐσμεν – τῶι χορηγεῖν διέφερον
καὶ τῆι] φιλοτιμίαι˙ κύνας παρέτρεφέ μοι,
ἵππους˙ ἐφυλάρχησα λαμπρῶς˙ τῶν φίλων   15
τοῖς δεομένοις τὰ μέτρι' ἐπαρκεῖν ἐδυνάμην.
δι' ἐκεῖνον ἦν ἄνθρωπος. ἀστείαν δ' ὅμως
τούτων χάριν τιν' ἀπεδίδουν˙ ἦν κόσμιος.
μετὰ τοῦτο συνέβη – καὶ γὰρ ἅμα τὰ πράγματα
ἡμῶν δίειμι πάντ'˙ ἄγω γάρ πως σχολήν –   20
Σαμίας ἑταίρας εἰς ἐπιθυμίαν τινὸς
ἐλθεῖν ἐκεῖνον, πρᾶγμ' ἴσως ἀνθρώπινον.
ἔκρυπτε τοῦτ', ἠισχύνετ'˙ ἠισθόμην ἐγὼ

14   παρέτρεφέ z: γαρέτρεφέ B
21   τινὸς z: τινα B
22   ἴσωσδε B

6

ACT ONE

[*The play begins with the entrance (presumably from Demeas'*
house) of Moskhion. He has not been speaking for long when
the papyrus starts up.]

MOSKHION:
    . . . why should I upset myself? . . . it's painful, since I did
wrong. I reckon it will be painful, but the most reasonable   5
thing I can do for you is to tell you all about my father's
character. I remember well, but pass over now, the life I led
after that, when I was a child. His benefactions then were
given when I was too young to appreciate them properly.
After I was enrolled into my deme, just like anyone else,   10
'one of the crowd' as they say, but, my word, much un-
luckier by nature – I can say this because we are by our-
selves – I outdid everyone acting as a *khorēgos* and in
displays of generosity. He kept hounds and horses for me.   15
I led my *phȳle* with distinction. I was able to give a little
help to my friends when they asked me. Because of him I
was a human being. But I gave him a fine return: I was
well-behaved. After this it happened – I'll go through all
of our affairs together: I have the time – it happened that   20
he fell in love with a certain Samian courtesan. It could
have happened, I think, to anyone. He tried to keep it dark:
he was ashamed. Even so I got to know,

ἄκοντος αὐτοῦ διελογιζόμην ϑ' ὅτι
ἂν μὴ γένηται τῆς ἑταίρας ἐγκρατής,   25
ὑπ' ἀντεραστῶν μειρακίων ἐνοχλήσεται,
τοῦτο <δὲ> ποῆσαι δι' ἔμ' ἴσως αἰσχύνεται
εἶσ]ω λαβεῖν ταύτην τὸ μὲν..[.]..π.[
...].οσε.[.].[

                    ].φέροντ' ἰδὼν
               ]..τος προσετίϑην πανταχοῦ
               ].ησϑε πρὸς τὸν γείτονα
               ]α συνϑλάσας τὸ σημεῖον σφόδρα
            φ]ιλανϑρώπως δὲ πρὸς τὴν τοῦ πατρὸς   35
Σαμί]αν διέκειϑ' ἡ τῆς κόρης μήτηρ, τά τε
πλεῖστ' ἦν παρ' αὐταῖς ἦδε, καὶ πάλιν ποτὲ
αὗται παρ' ἡμῖν. ἐξ ἀγροῦ δὴ καταδραμὼν
ὡς ἔτυ]χ[έ] γ' εἰς Ἀδώνι' αὐτὰς κατέλαβον
συνηγμένας ἐνθάδε πρὸς ἡμᾶς μετά τινων   40
ἄλλων γυναικῶν· τῆς δ' ἑορτῆς παιδιὰν
πολλὴ]ν ἐχούσης οἷον εἰκός, συμπαρὼν
ἐγινόμην οἶμαι θεατής· ἀγρυπνίαν
ὁ θόρυβος αὐτῶν ἐνεπόει γάρ μοι τινά·
ἐπὶ τὸ τέγος κήπους γὰρ ἀνέφερόν τινας,   45
ὠρχο]ῦντ', ἐπαννύχιζον ἐσκεδασμέναι.
ὀκνῶ λέγειν τὰ λοίπ', ἴσως δ' αἰσχύνομαι
ὅτ'] οὐδὲν ὄφελός ἐσθ'· ὅμως αἰσχύνομαι.

43   οἶμαι z: οἴμε B

48   αλλ'
     ομως B

8

although he didn't want me to, and I reckoned that if he   25
didn't get control of the girl he would have trouble from
younger rivals. However, he was ashamed, because of me
perhaps . . . to take the girl in . . .

       about 23 lines are missing

seeing him carrying/bearing . . .? I contributed/sided with —
everywhere — . . . (if/so that) you . . . to the neighbour   35
. . . smashing the seal . . . the girl's mother became friendly
with my father's Samian and she was often in their house
and in turn they used to visit us. Coming back in a hurry
from our farm I found them, as it happened, gathered at our
house for the Adonis-festival along with some other women.   40
The festivities, as one might expect, were providing a good
deal of fun and since I was there along with them I became
a sort of spectator. The noise they were making was giving
me a sleepless night — they were carrying their gardens on   45
to the roof, dancing, celebrating the night away, scattered
all over the roof. I hesitate to say what happened next —
perhaps I'm ashamed when there is no good being ashamed;
even so, I'm ashamed.

ἐκύησεν ἡ παῖς· τοῦτο γὰρ φράσας λέγω
καὶ τὴν πρὸ τούτου πρᾶξιν. οὐκ ἠρνησάμην   50
τὴν αἰτίαν σχών, ἀλλὰ πρότερος ἐνέτυχον
τῆι μητρὶ τῆς κόρης, ὑπεσχόμην γαμεῖν
ἂν σ]υνεπανέλθηι ποθ' ὁ πατήρ, <ἐπ> ὤμοσα.
τὸ παιδίον γενόμενον εἴληφ' οὐ πάλαι·
ἀπὸ ταὐτομάτου δὲ συμβέβηκε καὶ μάλ' <εὖ>·   55
ἔτικτε]ν ἡ Χρυσίς· καλοῦμεν τοῦτο γὰρ
                                        ] ονεου πάλαι

[ΧΡΥΣΙΣ]
    σπουδῆι πρὸς ἡμᾶσ[
    ἐγὼ δ' ἀναμείνασ' ὅ τι λέγουσ' ἀ[κροάσομαι.   60

Μο.   ἑόρακας αὐτὸς τὸν πατέρα σύ, Παρμένων;

ΠΑΡΜΕΝΩΝ
    οὔκουν ἀκούεις; φημί.

(Μο.)   καὶ τὸν γείτονα;

(Πα.)
    πάρεισιν.

(Μο.)   εὖ γ' ἐπόησαν.

(Πα.)   ἀλλ' ὅπως ἔσει
    ἀνδρεῖος εὐθύς τ' ἐμβαλεῖς περὶ τοῦ γάμου
    λόγον.

(Μο.)   τίνα τρόπον; δειλὸς ἤδη γίνομαι   65

10

The girl became pregnant. By telling you this, I am also
saying what happened before. I did not deny that I was to   50
blame. I went first to the girl's mother and promised to
marry the girl if ever my father returned with his companion.
I swore an oath. Not long ago when the baby was born, I
took it into the house. As it happened, there was a lucky
coincidence. Khrysis had a baby - that's what we call her   55
. . . a while ago.

> [About 25 lines are missing. In them Moskhion finishes
> his narrative and exits towards the harbour. Khrysis
> emerges from Demeas' house soliloquizing and observes
> Moskhion returning in the company of Parmenon.]

KHRYSIS: . . . home in a hurry. I'll wait and hear what they
say.   60

> [Enter Moskhion and Parmenon: they do not observe
> Khrysis.]

MOSKHION: Did you see father yourself, Parmenon?

PARMENON: Haven't I told you? Yes.

MOSKHION: And his neighbour?

PARMENON: They've arrived.

MOSKHION: I'm glad.

PARMENON: But make sure you behave like a man and raise
the topic of the marriage right away.

MOSKHION: How? Now that the crunch has come I'm afraid.   65

ὡς πλησίον τὸ πρᾶγμα γέγονε.

(Πα.)   πῶς λέγεις;

(Μο.) αἰσχύνομαι τὸν πατέρα.

(Πα.)   τὴν δὲ παρθένον
ἣν ἠδίκηκας τήν τε ταύτης μητέρα
ὅπως - τρέμεις, ἀνδρόγυνε;

Χρ.   τί βοᾶς, δύσμορε;

Πα.   καὶ Χρυσὶς ἦν ἐνταῦθ'. ἐρωτᾶς δή με σὺ   70
τί βοῶ· γελοῖον· βούλομ' εἶναι τοὺς γάμους
ἤδη, πεπαῦσθαι τουτονὶ πρὸς ταῖς θύραις
κλάοντα ταύταις, μηδ' ἐκεῖν' ἀμνημονεῖν
ὧν ὤμοσεν· θύειν, στεφανοῦσθαι, σησαμῆν
κόπτειν· παρελθὼν αὐτός. οὐχ ἱκανὰς ἔχειν   75
προφάσεις δοκῶ σοι;

(Μο.)   πάντα ποιήσω· τί δεῖ
λέγειν;

(Χρ.)   ἐγὼ μὲν οἴομαι.

(Μο.)   τὸ παιδίον
οὕτως ἐῶμεν ὡς ἔχει ταύτην τρέφειν
αὐτήν τε φάσκειν τετοκέναι;

(Χρ.)   τί δὴ γὰρ οὔ;

75   κόπτειν παρελθὼν· Β
77   τοδε Β   παιδιονεχειν Β

12

PARMENON: What do you mean?

MOSKHION: I feel shame before my father.

PARMENON [*his voice rising*]: What about the girl you have
wronged? What about her mother? Just make sure — [*he
breaks off, noticing Moskhion's agitation*] you're shaking,
you! you're only half a man!

KHRYSIS [*interrupting*]: Why are you shouting, you wretch?

PARMENON [*reacting with surprise*]: So Khrysis is here too!   70
You ask me why I am shouting. It's ridiculous. I want the
wedding under way, I want this fellow here to stop weeping
by that door and not to forget that oath he swore when he
went in — I want sacrificing, garlands to be worn, cake cut-
ting. Don't you think I have plenty of reasons for shouting?   75

MOSKHION: I'll do everything. Of course I will.

KHRYSIS: I'm sure you will.

MOSKHION: Are we to let Khrysis bring up the baby just as
she is doing now and say that it is hers?

KHRYSIS: Of course.

(Mo.) ὁ πατὴρ χαλεπανεῖ σοι .

(Χρ.)   πεπαύσεται πάλιν,   80
    ἐραῖ γάρ, ὦ βέλτιστε, κἀκεῖνος κακῶς,
    οὐχ ἧττον ἢ σύ· τοῦτο δ' εἰς διαλλαγὰς
    ἄγει τάχιστα καὶ τὸν ὀργιλώτατον.
    πρότερον δ' ἔγωγε πάντ' ἂν ὑπομεῖναι δοκῶ
    ἢ τοῦτο τίτθην ἐν συνοικίαι τινὶ   85

[Μο.]   βούλομαι
                                 λά]βοις
                              γ]ὰρ ἀθλιώτερον   90
           ] πάντων· οὐκ ἀπάγξομαι ταχύ;
         ῥ]ήτωρ μόνος γὰρ φιλόφρονος.
       ]ότερός εἰμ' ἐν γε τοῖς νυνὶ λόγοις.
       ἀ]πελθὼν εἰς ἐρημίαν τινὰ
    γυμν]άζομ'· οὐ γὰρ μέτριος ἀγὼν ἐστί μοι.   95

[ΔΗΜΕΑΣ]
    οὔκουν μεταβολῆς αἰσθάνεσθ' ἤδη τόπου,
    ὅσον διαφέρει ταῦτα τῶν ἐκεῖ κακῶν;

<ΝΙΚΗΡΑΤΟΣ>
    Πόντος· παχεῖς γέροντες, ἰχθῦς ἄφθονοι,
    ἀηδία τις πραγμάτων. Βυζάντιον·
    ἀψίνθιον, πικρὰ πάντ'. Ἄπολλον. ταῦτα δὲ   100
    καθαρὰ πενήτων ἀγαθά.

<Δη.>   Ἀθῆναι φίλταται,

MOSKHION: Father will be angry with you.

KHRYSIS: And he will stop being angry again. He's in love, dear, and in a bad way, just like you. Love leads even the most irascible of men to make up very soon after a quarrel. But I'd put up with anything rather than ?see some wet-nurse bringing up the baby in a tenement . . . 80

[*About 23 lines are missing. Khrysis and Parmenon have gone into Demeas' house. Moskhion is left soliloquizing.*]

MOSKHION: I want . . . you would accept . . . more wretched . . . all . . . Why don't I hang myself right away? . . . a single speaker (?a speaker who alone) . . . of a well-disposed person. ?I'm more nervous in the present debate. I'm going off on my own to practise my speech. No mean struggle lies ahead. 90

95

[*He exits down one of the side entrances. After a moment Demeas, Nikeratos and some slaves carrying baggage enter from the side entrance that leads to the Peiraieus.*]

DEMEAS [*to Nikeratos and the slaves*]: You must notice the change of place now? What a difference between here and the discomforts there!

NIKERATOS: The Pontos. Rich old men. Lots of fish. Business all unpleasant. Byzantion. Wormwood. Everything sour. But, my word, here there is nothing but pure benefit for poor folk. 100

DEMEAS: Dear Athens,

πῶς ἂν γένοιθ' ὑμῖν ὅσων ἔστ' ἄξιαι,
ἵν' ὦμεν ἡμεῖς πάντα μακαριώτατοι
οἱ τὴν πόλιν φιλοῦντες. – εἴσω παράγετε
ὑμεῖς. ἀπόπληχθ', ἕστηκας ἐμβλέπων ἐμοί;   105

Νι. ἐκεῖν' ἐθαύμαζον μάλιστα, Δημέα,
τῶν περὶ ἐκεῖνον τὸν τόπον· τὸν ἥλιον
οὐκ ἦν ἰδεῖν ἐνίοτε παμπόλλου χρόνου·
ἀὴρ παχύς τις, ὡς ἔοικ', ἐπεσκότει.

(Δη.) οὔκ, ἀλλὰ σεμνὸν οὐδὲν ἐθεᾶτ' αὐτόθι,   110
ὥστ' αὐτὰ τἀναγκαῖ' ἐπέλαμπε τοῖς ἐκεῖ.

(Νι.) νὴ τὸν Διόνυσον, εὖ λέγεις.

<Δη.>   καὶ ταῦτα μὲν
ἑτέροις μέλειν ἐῶμεν· ὑπὲρ ὧν δ' ἐλέγομεν
τί δοκεῖ ποεῖν σοι;

(Νι.)   τὰ περὶ τὸν γάμον λέγεις
τῶι μειρακίωι σου;

(Δη.)   πάνυ γε.

<Νι.>   ταῦτ' ἀεὶ λέγω.   115
ἀγαθῆι τύχηι πράττωμεν, ἡμέραν τινὰ
θέμενοι.

(Δη.)   δέδοκται ταῦτα;

<Νι.>   ἐμοὶ γοῦν.

(Δη.)   ἀλλὰ μὴν

I wish you the blessings you deserve so that we, who love
our city, may be completely happy. [*He turns to the slaves.*]
Inside you! [*They set off. One of them dawdles.*] You
numbskull, why do you stand there gawping at me? [*This*   105
slave hurriedly departs.]

NIKERATOS: [*resuming his train of thought*]: I'll tell you
what surprised me most of all about that place, Demeas.
Sometimes there were long periods when you couldn't see
the sun. A kind of thick mist was obscuring it, I suppose.

DEMEAS: Yes. There was nothing worth seeing there. That's   110
why the locals had the bare minimum of light.

NIKERATOS: My word, you're right.

DEMEAS: Let's leave this for others to think about. Apropos
of the matter we were discussing. What do you think should
be done?

NIKERATOS: You mean about your boy's marriage?

DEMEAS: Yes.

NIKERATOS: I haven't changed my mind. Let's fix a day   115
and get on with it. And good luck to us!

DEMEAS: That's what you've decided?

NIKERATOS: *I* have.

DEMEAS: Well,

κἀμοὶ προτέρωι σου.

(Νι.)   παρακάλει μ' ὅταν ἐξίηις.

(Δη.)   ὀλ] ίγα στ [

[ΧΟΡΟΥ]

I decided this before you did.

NIKERATOS: Ask for me when you go out.

DEMEAS: . . . a few . . .

> [*About 14 lines are lost. The old men enter their houses,
> the one who is last to leave having observed a band of
> drunken young revellers (see the introduction, p.xv)
> who enter and then perform*
>
> THE FIRST CHORAL INTERLUDE]

ΜΕΡΟΣ Β

[ΜΟΣΧΙΩΝ]

      ]ντο εἰ καὶ δι.[   ].ν   120
ἐ]γὼ μελετήσας ὧν τό[τ' ἐνόουν..]..μαι.
ὡς ἐγενόμην γὰρ ἐκτὸ[ς ἄστεως μ]όνος,
ἔθυον, ἐπὶ τὸ δεῖπνον [ἐκάλουν τοὺς φίλ]ους,
ἐπὶ λούτρ' ἔπεμπον τὰς γ[υναῖκας,] περιπατῶν

τὴν σησαμῆν διένεμον, η[......]οτε   125
ὑμέναιον ἐτερέτιζον· ἦν ἀβέλτερος·
ὡς δ' οὖν ἐνεπλήσθην – ἀλλ', Ἄπολλον, οὑτοσὶ
ὁ πατήρ. ἀκήκο' ἄρα. χαῖρέ μοι, πάτερ.

(Δη.) νὴ καὶ σύ γ', ὦ παῖ.

(Μο.)   τί σκυθρωπάζεις;

(Δη.)   τί γάρ;
γαμετὴν ἑταίραν, ὡς ἔοικ', ἐλάνθανον   130
ἔχων.

(Μο.)   γαμετήν; πῶς; ἀγνοῶ <γὰρ> τὸν λόγον.

(Δη.) λάθ]ριό[ς τι]ς ὑός, ὡς ἔοικε, γέγονέ μοι.

    ...]ἐς κόρακας ἄπεισιν ἐκ τῆς οἰκίας
ἤ]δη λαβ[ο]ῦσα.

(Μο.)   μηδαμῶς.

(Δη.)   πῶς μηδαμῶς;

ACT TWO

[Enter Demeas from his house soliloquizing. He does not notice Moskhion coming in from one of the side entrances. When the papyrus resumes Moskhion is soliloquizing (he cannot have been speaking for long).]

MOSKHION:

  . . . having practised (none of the arguments I meant to)
  . . . Since, when I was by myself outside the city, I began
  the sacrifice, I invited my friends to the meal, I sent off the
  women to fetch the sacral water. I divided the cake, some-
  times I hummed the wedding hymn. I was a complete fool.   125
  Well, when I had had my fill of this — *[turning round and*
  observing Demeas, he breaks off] Goodness! It's father.
  He must have heard, Hallo, father.
DEMEAS: Hallo, son.
MOSKHION: Why do you look so glum?
DEMEAS: You ask? It seems I didn't know I had a mistress
  who was also a wife.   130
MOSKHION: A wife? What do you mean? I don't under-
  stand what you say.
DEMEAS: It seems a son has been born to me in secret. Well,
  she will leave the house with the boy and good riddance to
  her!
MOSKHION: No! No!
DEMEAS: What do you mean 'no'?

21

ἀλλ' ἦ με θρέψειν ἔνδον ὑὸν προσδοκᾷς   135
νόθον; [.....]ν γ' οὐ τοῦ τρόπου τοὐμοῦ λέγεις.

(Μο.) τίς δ' ἐστιν ἡμῶν γνήσιος, πρὸς τῶν θεῶν,
ἢ τίς νόθος, γενόμενος ἄνθρωπος;

(Δη.)   σὺ μὲν
παίζεις.

(Μο.)   μὰ τὸν Διόνυσον, <ἀλλ'> ἐσπούδακα·
οὐθὲν γένος γένους γὰρ οἶμαι διαφέρειν,   140
ἀλλ' εἰ δικαίως ἐξετάσαι τις, γνήσιος
ὁ χρηστός ἐστιν, ὁ δὲ πονηρὸς καὶ νόθος

[Δη.]   ]ἐσπούδακας.   145

(Μο.)   ]ν γαμεῖν ἐρῶ
                               ]ν μὴ τοὺς γάμους

          [Δη.]   ].ως, παῖ.

(Μο.)   βούλομαι
                          ]δοκεῖν

(Δη.)   καλῶς ποεῖς.

135   ἀλλ' ἦ z: αλλω o²[B]
140   Stob.Ecl.iv.29.10 = fr. 248 K-T
      ]σγενους B: γένους γένος Stob.
      ἐξετάσεις καὶ γνησίως Stob.
142   οχρηστοσε[o²   ]επονηρος B

22

Do you really expect me to bring up a bastard son? That's   135
not at all in my line.

MOSKHION [*pompously*] But who is legitimate, pray tell me,
and who illegitimate if he is born a man?

DEMEAS: You're joking.

MOSKHION: No. I'm quite serious. I do not believe there   140
are distinctions of birth. If one were to examine the matter
fairly, the good man is true-born, the villain illegitimate as
well . . .

> [*Ten mutilated verses follow, then a lacuna of about*
> *sixteen lines.*]

DEMEAS: . . . you're serious.   145

MOSKHION: ?to marry: I'm in love . . . in case . . . the
wedding.

DEMEAS: . . . son.

MOSKHION: I want . . . to seem . . .

DEMEAS: Well done!

(Μο.)

        [Δη.]..ᾶν διδῶσ' οὗτοι, γαμεῖς.   150

(Μο.) πῶς ἄν, π]υθόμενος μηδὲ ἓν τοῦ πράγματος,
      ἐσπουδακότα μ' αἴσθοιο συλλάβοις τέ μοι;

(Δη.) ἐσπουδακότα; μηδὲν πυθόμενος; καταν[οῶ
      τὸ πρᾶγμα, Μοσχίων, ὃ λέγεις· ἤδη τρέχω
      πρὸς τουτονὶ καὶ τοὺς γάμους αὐτῶι φράσω   155
      ποεῖν· τὰ παρ' ἡμῶν γὰρ παρέσται ταῦ[
      λέγεις περιρρανάμενος ἤδη παρα[γαγών,
      σπείσας τε καὶ λιβανωτὸν ἐπιθείς –

[Μο.]   [τὴν κόρην
      μέτειμι.

(Δη.)   μήπω δὴ βάδιζ', ἄχ[ρι ἂν μάθω
      εἰ ταῦτα συγχωρήσεθ' ἡμῖ[ν   160

(Μο.) οὐκ ἀντερεῖ σοι· παρενοχλε[ῖν δ'
      ἐμὲ συμπαρόντ' ἔστ' ἀπρε[πές

(Δη.) ταὐτόματόν ἐστιν ὡς ἔοικέ που θεὸς
      σωίζει τε πολλὰ τῶν ἀοράτων πραγμάτων·
      ἐγὼ γὰρ οὐκ εἰδὼς ἔχον[τα τουτονὶ   165
      ἐρωτικῶς, ταῦ[τ'

(Δη.)   Παρμένων, παῖ, Παρμένων,
      στε]φάνους, ἱερεῖον, σήσαμα 190
      ]πάντα τὰξ ἀγορᾶς ἀπλῶς

MOSKHION: . . .

DEMEAS: If they offer the girl, you'll marry her? 150

MOSKHION: Can't you see without asking questions that I
am serious? Can't you accept my cooperation?

DEMEAS: 'Serious'? 'Without asking questions'? I understand, Moskhion. I'm running to Nikeratos already. I'll tell 155
him to start the wedding. Our part of the ceremony will be
ready . . . you say. I'll go in and sprinkle myself with water,
pour a libation and put the incense on the altar and then –
[Moskhion interrupts]

MOSKHION: I'll fetch the girl.

DEMEAS: Not yet, not before I make sure whether Nikeratos
will agree.

MOSKHION: He won't oppose you. In any case it's out of 160
place for me to be here and in the way (of the preparations).
[Moskhion exits.]

DEMEAS: [left alone] It seems that the accidental is indeed
a divinity and looks after many of the things we cannot
see. Not knowing Moskhion was in love, I . . . 165
[After a lacuna of about 27 lines the papyrus resumes
in the middle of an extremely fragmentary conversation
between Nikeratos and Demeas. In the course of this
there is talk of 'fixing a day' and then of 'today' (twice),
of 'impossibility', 'agreement', 'being sensible': the dialogue then becomes more intelligible:]

DEMEAS: Parmenon! Parmenon! . . . garlands, a sacrificial
beast, sesame seeds . . quite simply everything we need from
market.

πριάμενος ἦ]κε.

(Πα.)   πάντ'; ἐμοὶ <   > Δημέα
          ] αλίπηι.

(Δη.)   καὶ ταχέως˙ ἤδη λέγω.
          ἄγε καὶ μ]άγειρον.

(Πα.)   καὶ μάγειρον; πριάμενος
          τᾶλλα;

(Δη.)   π]ριάμενος.

(Πα.)   ἀργύριον λαβὼν τρέχω.   195

(Δη.) σὺ δ' οὐδ]έπω, Νικήρατε;

(Νι.)   εἰσιὼν φράσας
          πρὸς τὴν γυναῖκα τἄνδον εὐτρεπῆ ποεῖν
          διώξομ' εὐθὺς τοῦτον.

(Πα.)   οὐκ οἶδ' οὐδὲ ἕν,
          πλὴν προστέτακται ταῦτα συντείνω τ' ἐκεῖ
          ἤδη.

Δη.   τὸ πεῖσαι τὴν γυναῖκα πράγματα   200
          αὐτῶι παρέξει˙ δεῖ δὲ μὴ δοῦναι λόγον
          μηδὲ χρόνον ἡ[μ]ᾶς. παῖ, διατρίβεις. οὐ δραμεῖ;
                    ]ρος ἡ γυνὴ
                    ]ἱκετεύω˙ τί οὖν;

          [ΧΟΡΟΥ]

                    26

Come back when you've bought it all.   190

PARMENON [*who must have entered in answer to the call*]:
  'Everything'? Me . . . Demeas . . . neglects?

DEMEAS: And hurry up! I tell you now. Bring a cook as
  well.

PARMENON: A cook as well? Once I've bought the other
  things?

DEMEAS: Yes.

PARMENON: I'll get the money and be off [*exits into Demeas'*   195
  house].

DEMEAS: You're not on your way yet, Nikeratos?

NIKERATOS: I'll go in and tell my wife to get the house
  ready. Then I'll follow this fellow [*exits into his house*].

PARMENON [*re-entering with a shopping-basket and speaking
  back into the house*]: I haven't a clue what's going on,
  except I've been given orders and I'm trying to carry them
  out at once.

DEMEAS [*soliloquizing*]: He'll have a job persuading his   200
  wife. We mustn't spend time on explanations. [*Turning to
  Parmenon*] Boy, you're holding us up. Get a move on . . .
  his wife . . . I beg you . . . what then?

   [*About ten lines are missing in the course of which
   Parmenon must set out for the market, Nikeratos come
   out of his house and follow him and Demeas go back into
   his house. There will have followed*

THE SECOND CHORAL INTERLUDE]

27

[ΔΗΜΕΑΣ]   ]. δρόμου καλοῦ
χειμὼν ἀπροσδόκητος ἐξαίφνης [
ἐλθών· ἐκεῖνος τοὺς ἐν εὐδίαι ποτὲ
θέοντας ἐξήραξε κάνεχαίτισεν.
τοιοῦτο γὰρ καὶ τοὐμόν ἐστι νῦν· ἐγὼ   210
ὁ τοὺς γάμους ποῶν, ὁ θύων τοῖς θεοῖς,
ὧι πάντα κατὰ νοῦν ἀρτίως ἐγίγνετο,
οὐδ' εἰ βλέπω, μὰ τὴν Ἀθηνᾶν, οἶδ[α νῦν
καλῶς ἔτ'· οὐκ, ἀλλ' εἰς τὸ πρόσθεν π[ροάγομαι,
πληγ]ήν τιν' ἀνυπέρβλητον ἐξ[αίφνης λαβών.   215
ἦ στ[ι] πιθανόν; σκέψασθε πότερο[ν εὖ φρονῶ   (Ι)
ἢ μαίνομ', οὐδέν τ' εἰς ἀκρίβειαν [τότε
λαβὼν ἐπάγομαι μέγ' ἀτύχημα [
ὡς γὰρ τάχιστ' εἰσῆλθον, ὑπερεσπουδακὼς
τὰ τοῦ γάμου πράττειν, φράσας τὸ πρᾶγμ' ἁπλῶς   220
τοῖς ἔνδον ἐκέλευσ' εὐτρεπίζειν πάνθ' ἃ δεῖ,   (6)
καθαρὰ ποεῖν, πέττειν, ἐνάρχεσθαι κανοῦν.
ἐγίνετ' ἀμέλει πάνθ' ἑτοίμως, τὸ δὲ τάχος
τῶν πραττομένων ταραχήν τιν' αὐτοῖς ἐνεπόει,
ὅπερ εἰκός. ἐπὶ κλίνης μὲν ἔρριπτ' ἐκποδὼν   225
τὸ παιδίον κεκραγός· αἱ δ' ἐβόων ἅμα   (ΙΙ)
"ἄλευρ', ὕδωρ, ἔλαιον ἀπόδος, ἄνθρακας."
καὐτὸς διδοὺς τούτων τι καὶ συλλαμβάνων
εἰς τὸ ταμιεῖον ἔτυχον εἰσελθών, ὅθεν
πλείω προαιρῶν καὶ σκοπούμενος [230
οὐκ εὐθὺς ἐξῆλθον. καθ' ὃν δ' ἦν χρόνον ἐγὼ   (16)

209 ἐξήραξε καὶ ἀνεχαίτισεν Favorinus, de exilio
    col. 23.27 = fr. 701 K.-T.
225 ευθυσεκποδῶ C [B]

ACT THREE

[*Demeas has entered from his house and has just begun
speaking.*]

DEMEAS:

 . . . a fair voyage . . . an unexpected storm, suddenly
coming. It has smashed and capsized mariners who were a
moment ago running on a calm sea. Such is the case with   210
me. I, who was starting the wedding, sacrificing to the gods,
I, for whom everything was going according to plan, now no
longer know if I am still seeing straight. I am brought
out to you, the victim of an unsurpassable blow. Can one   215
believe it? Consider whether I'm sane or mad, whether by
not ascertaining the exact truth, I'm bringing a great misfortune upon myself.

 As soon as I went in, because I was extremely keen to
get the wedding in progress, I explained everything quite
simply to my household and told them to get ready every-   220
thing that was needed, to clean the house, to bake, to
'inaugurate' the basket. All was going well, but the speed
of things was causing some disturbance, as one might expect.
The baby had been dumped out of the way on a couch and   225
was crying. The women were shouting all at once 'Flour!
Water! Oil! Charcoal!' I myself, supplying one or other of
these and helping out, happened to have gone into the store
room and, because I was picking out more things and exam-
ining . . . had not come out straightaway. Meanwhile   230

ἐνταῦθα, κατέβαιν' ἀφ' ὑπερῴου τις γυνὴ
ἄνωθεν εἰς τοὔμπροσθε τοῦ ταμιειδίου
οἴκημα· τυγχάνει γὰρ ἱστεών τις ὤν,
ὥσθ' ἥ τ' ἀνάβασίς ἐστι διὰ τούτου τό τε   235
ταμιεῖον ἡμῖν. τοῦ δὲ Μοσχίωνος ἦν   (21)
τίτθη τις αὕτη, πρεσβυτέρα, γεγονυῖ' ἐμὴ
θεράπαιν', ἐλευθέρα δὲ νῦν. ἰδοῦσα δὲ
τὸ παιδίον κεκραγὸς ἠμελημένον
ἐμέ τ' οὐδὲν εἰδυῖ' ἔνδον ὄντ', ἐν ἀσφαλεῖ   240
εἶναι νομίσασα τοῦ λαλεῖν, προσέρχεται   (26)
καὶ ταῦτα δὴ τὰ κοινὰ "φίλτατον τέκνον"
εἰποῦσα καὶ "μέγ' ἀγαθόν· ἡ μάμμη δὲ ποῦ;"
ἐφίλησε, περιήνεγκεν. ὡς δ' ἐπαύσατο
κλᾶον, πρὸς αὐτήν φησιν " ὦ τάλαιν' ἐγώ,   245
πρώην τοιοῦτον ὄντα Μοσχίων' ἐγὼ   (31)
αὐτὸν ἐτιθηνούμην ἀγαπῶσα, νῦν δ' ἐπεὶ
παιδίον ἐκείνου γέγονεν ἤδη καὶ τόδε

                    ]α καὶ
                γεγο]νέναι."   250
        ]καὶ θεραπαινιδίωι τινὶ   (36)
ἔξωθεν εἰστρέχοντι, "λούσατ', ὦ τάλαν,
τὸ παιδίον" φησίν, "τί τοῦτ'; ἐν τοῖς γάμοις
τοῖς τοῦ πατρὸς τὸν μικρὸν οὐ θεραπεύετε;"
εὐθὺς δ' ἐκείνη "δύσμορ', ἡλίκον λαλεῖς"   255
φήσ'· "ἔνδον ἐστὶν αὐτός." "οὐ δήπου γε· ποῦ;" (41)
"ἐν τῶι ταμιείωι", καὶ παρεξήλλαξέ τι·
"αὐτὴ καλεῖ τίτθη σε" καὶ "βάδιζε καὶ
σπεῦδ'· οὐκ ἀκήκο' οὐδέν· εὐτυχέστατα."

a woman came downstairs into the room directly in front of
the store-room – you see there happens to be a weaving-
room through which you have to go if you want to go up-   235
stairs or if you want to go to the store-room. This was
Moskhion's old nurse, quite old now – she was once my
slave – and free. When she saw the child was left on its
own and was crying, not knowing I was in earshot, she
thought she could talk quite safely. So she went up to the
child, saying all the usual things 'dear, dear baby', 'little   240
treasure' 'where's mummy?' and kissed it and started
carrying it around. When it stopped crying, she said to
herself 'Dear me! Not so long ago I was lovingly nursing
Moskhion himself – he was just like this one – and now
since this baby of his has been born . . .

   [*Two or three lines are missing and only the ends of the*
   three following lines survive. Demeas is now speaking in
   propria persona.]

. . . when some serving-girl came in, she said to her 'Bath
the baby. Dearie me! What is going on. When a father's
being married, you don't look after the little one?'
Immediately the girl replies, 'Wretched woman! How loudly
you are talking! The master's in here'. 'Not really? Where?   255
'In the store-room'. Here the girl stopped whispering and
said loudly 'Mistress is calling you, nurse' and 'Go on, get
a move on: he hasn't heard anything. It's all right'.

εἰποῦσ' ἐκείνη δ' "ὦ τάλαινα τῆς ἐμῆς   260
λαλιᾶς", ἀπῆῖξεν ἐκποδών, οὐκ οἶδ' ὅποι.   (46)
κἀγὼ προῃίειν τοῦτον ὅνπερ ἐνθάδε
τρόπον ἀρτίως ἐξῆλθον, ἡσυχῇ πάνυ,
ὡς οὔτ' ἀκούσας οὐδὲν οὔτ' ἠισθημένος.
αὐτὴν δ' ἔχουσαν αὐτὸ τὴν Σαμίαν ὁρῶ   265
ἔξω καθ' αὑτὴν <καὶ> διδοῦσαν τιτθίον   (51)
ὥσθ' ὅτι μὲν αὐτῆς ἐστι τοῦτο γνώριμον
εἶναι, πατρὸς δ' ὅτου ποτ' ἐστίν, εἴτ' ἐμὸν
εἴτ' – οὐ λέγω δ', ἄνδρες, πρὸς ὑμᾶς τοῦτ' ἐγώ,
οὐχ ὑπονοῶ, τὸ πρᾶγμα δ' εἰς μέσον φέρω   270
ἅ τ' ἀκήκο' αὐτός, οὐκ ἀγανακτῶν οὐδέπω.   (56)
σύνοιδα γὰρ τῶι μειρακίωι, νὴ τοὺς θεούς,
καὶ κοσμίωι τὸν πρότερον ὄντι χρόνον ἀεὶ
καὶ περὶ ἔμ' ὡς ἔνεστιν εὐσεβεστάτωι.
πάλιν δ', ἐπειδὰν τὴν λέγουσαν καταμάθω   275
τίτθην ἐκείνου πρῶτον οὖσαν, εἶτ' ἐμοῦ   (61)
λάθραι λέγουσαν, εἶτ' ἀποβλέψω πάλιν
εἰς τὴν ἀγαπῶσαν αὐτὸ καὶ βεβιασμένην
ἐμοῦ τρέφειν ἄκοντος, ἐξέστηχ' ὅλως.
ἀλλ' εἰς καλὸν γὰρ τουτονὶ παρόνθ' ὁρῶ   280
τὸν Παρμένοντ' ἐκ τῆς ἀγορᾶς· ἐατέον   (66)
αὐτὸν παραγαγεῖν ἐστι τούτους οὓς ἄγει.

261 απηλθεν C
262 κωγωπροηλθον C
266 ἔξω διδοῦσαν τιτθίον παριὼν ἅμα C
267 εστιτουτοαυτης BC
270 εισμεσον C: εσομενον B
280 τουτονε[..]ρονθ C: τουτονιπροσιονθ B

The nurse cried 'Ah me! What a blabberer I am!' and   260
darted off, god knows where.

    I came forth then just as you saw me come out here a
little while ago, quite calmly as though I hadn't heard or
seen anything. As I was coming out I saw my Samian
holding the baby and offering it her breast. That makes it   265
quite clear who is the baby's mother but as for the father,
whether the baby's mine or — but this I won't say to you,
gentlemen, nor do I suspect it. I'm just bringing into the   270
open what I have heard. I'm not angry, not yet. I know
the boy, I do. He was always well-behaved and as dutiful
to his father as he could be. But then — whenever I reckon
that the woman who was talking was his own nurse and that   275
she talked when she thought I wasn't there and whenever I
look back at Khrysis who adores the child and who forced
me to raise it when I didn't want to — I am quite beside
myself.

    [*He sees Parmenon coming in by one of the side-entrances*
    with the cook and his entourage.]

Good! I see Parmenon here, back from market. I'll let him   280
take these people in.

33

Πα.   μάγειρ', ἐγώ, μὰ τοὺς θεούς, οὐκ οἶδα σὺ
      ἐφ' ὅ τι μαχαίρας περιφέρεις· ἱκανὸς γὰρ εἶ
      λαλῶν κατακόψαι πάντα πράγματα.

(ΜΑΓΕΙΡΟΣ)   ἄθλιε   285
      ἰδιῶτα.

(Πα.)   ἐγώ;

(Μα.)   δοκεῖς γέ μοι, νὴ τοὺς θεούς.   (71)
      εἰ πυνθάνομαι πόσας τραπέζας μέλλετε
      ποεῖν, πόσαι γυναῖκές εἰσι, πηνίκα
      ἔσται τὸ δεῖπνον, εἰ δεήσει προσλαβεῖν
      τραπεζοποιόν, εἰ κέραμός ἐστ' ἔνδοθεν   290
      ὑμῖν ἱκανός, εἰ τοὐπτάνιον κατάστεγον,   (76)
      εἰ τἄλλ' ὑπάρχει πάντα –

(Πα.)   κατακόπτεις γέ με,
      εἰ λανθάνει σε, φίλτατ', εἰς περικόμματα,
      οὐχ ὡς ἔτυχεν.

(Μα.)   οἴμωζε.

(Πα.)   καὶ σύ, τοῦτό γε
      πάντος ἕνεκ'. ἀλλὰ παράγετ' εἴσω.

Δη.   Παρμένων.   295

(Πα.) ἐμέ τις κέκληκε;

294   ετυχες Β
295   παραγ' Β

34

[*He stands aside so that the new entrants do not see him.*]

PARMENON: Damn it, cook! I don't know why you carry around knives with you. You're quite capable on your own of chopping everything up with your chatter.

COOK: You don't know the trade, poor fellow! 285

PARMENON: You mean me?

COOK: That's what I think you are. When I ask about the number of tables, how many women there are, the time of the meal, whether I'll need to bring along a table-layer, whether 290 you have enough plate in the house, whether the kitchen is under cover, if everything else is ready —

PARMENON: In case you don't notice, my dear fellow, you are chopping me up into small pieces — and very artfully.

COOK: Damn you!

PARMENON: And you, on every count! But in with you all. 295

[*The Cook and his attendants go in: before he can follow them, Parmenon is detained by Demeas.*]

DEMEAS: Parmenon!

PARMENON: Someone calling me?

(Δη.)   ναίχι.

(Πα.)   χαῖρε, δέσποτα.   (81)

(Δη.) τὴν σφυρίδα καταθεὶς ἧκε δεῦρο.

(Πα.)   ἀγαθῆι τύχηι.

(Δη.) τοῦτον γὰρ οὐδέν, ὡς ἐγῶιμαι, λανθάνοι
       τοιοῦτον ἂν πραττόμενον ἔργον· ἔστι γὰρ
       περίεργος, εἴ τις ἄλλος. ἀλλὰ τὴν θύραν   300
       προϊὼν πέπληχε.

(Πα.)   δίδοτε, Χρυσί, πάνθ' ὅσ' ἂν (86)
       ὁ μάγειρος αἰτῆι, τὴν δὲ γραῦν φυλάττετε
       ἀπὸ τῶν κεραμίων, πρὸς θεῶν. τί δεῖ ποεῖν,
       δέσποτα;

(Δη.)   τί δεῖ ποεῖν <σε>; δεῦρ' ἀπὸ τῆς θύρας·
       ἔτι μικρόν.

(Πα.)   ἦν.

(Δη.)   ἄκουε δή νυν, Παρμένων·   305
       ἐγώ σε μαστιγοῦν, μὰ τοὺς δώδεκα θεούς,   (91)
       οὐ βούλομαι διὰ πολλά.

(Πα.)   μαστιγοῦν; τί δὲ
       πεπόηκα;

296   καλει C
305   νυν C: μου B

36

DEMEAS: Yes.

PARMENON: Hello, master.

DEMEAS: Come back here once you've put down the basket.

PARMENON: Fine! [*He enters the house.*]

DEMEAS: I'm quite sure nothing could get past this man,
nothing of the kind of thing I'm concerned with. He's a
busybody if anyone is. He's coming out, banging the door. 300

> [*Parmenon enters, speaking back into the house*]

PARMENON: Make sure, Khrysis, that you give the cook
everything he asks for and keep the old woman away from
the pottery, please.

> [*He turns round confidently and addresses Demeas.*]
What's to do, master?

DEMEAS: You ask? Come this way, away from the door.
Come on, a little further.

PARMENON: There.

DEMEAS: Listen now, Parmenon. There are many reasons 305
why I don't want to beat you.

PARMENON: Beat me? What have I done?

(Δη.)   συγκρύπτεις τι πρός μ', ἤσθημαι.

[Πα.]   ἐγώ;
      μὰ τὸν Διόνυσον, μὰ τὸν Ἀπόλλω τουτονί,
      μὰ τὸν Δία τὸν Σωτῆρα, μὰ τὸν Ἀσκληπιόν -   310

(Δη.) παῦ· μηδὲν ὄμνυ'· οὐ γὰρ εἰκάζων λέγω.   (96)

(Πα.) ἦ μήποτ' ἄρα -

(Δη.)   οὗτος, βλέπε δεῦρο.

(Πα.)   ἰδού, βλέπω.

(Δη.) τὸ παιδίον τίνος ἐστίν;

(Πα.)   ἦν.

(Δη.)   τὸ παιδίον
      τίνος ἐστ' ἐρωτῶ.

(Πα.)   Χρυσίδος.

(Δη.)   πατρὸς δὲ τοῦ;

(Πα.) σόν, φ[ησιν].

[Δη.]   ἀπόλωλας· φενακίζεις με.

(Πα.)   ἐγώ;   315

(Δη.) εἰδότα γ' ἀκριβῶς πάντα καὶ πεπυσμένον   (101)

308   προσμ' C: πραγμ' B   ἐγὼ init. 309 ponit C[B]
313   ἦν z: ην CB

38

DEMEAS: You and the others are keeping something from
    me. I know.

PARMENON: By Dionysos, by Apollo here, by Zeus Sōtēr,
    by Asklepios —   310

DEMEAS: That's enough. No oaths. I am not making guesses.

PARMENON: Else may I never —

DEMEAS: You there, look this way.

PARMENON: There: I'm looking.

DEMEAS: Whose is the baby?

PARMENON: Ah!

DEMEAS: I'm asking you. Whose is the child?

PARMENON: It belongs to Khrysis.

DEMEAS: And its father?

PARMENON: She says it's yours.

DEMEAS: You're done for. You're trying to trick me.

PARMENON: Me?   315

DEMEAS: I know all the details. I've found out that it's
    Moskhion's baby, that you know all about it

ὅτι Μοσχίωνός ἐστιν, ὅτι σύνοισθα σύ,
ὅτι δι' ἐκεῖνον αὐτὸ νῦν αὕτη τρέφει.

(Πα.) τίς φησι;

(Δη.)   πάντες. ἀλλ' ἀπόκριναι τοῦτό μοι·
ταῦτ' ἐστίν;

(Πα.)   ἔστι, δέσποτ', ἀλλὰ λανθάνειν - 320

(Δη.) τί "λανθάνειν"; ἱμάντα παίδων τις δότω   (106)
ἐπὶ τουτονί μοι τὸν ἀσεβῆ.

(Πα.)   μή, πρὸς θεῶν.

(Δη.) στίξω σε, νὴ τὸν Ἥλιον.

(Πα.)   στίξεις ἐμέ;

(Δη.) ἤδη γε.

(Πα.)   ἀπόλωλα.

(Δη.)   ποῖ σύ, ποῖ, μαστιγία;
λάβ' αὐτόν. ὦ πόλισμα Κεκροπίας χθονός,   325
ὦ ταναὸς αἰθήρ, ὦ - τί, Δημέα, βοᾷς;   (111)
τί βοᾷς, ἀνόητε; κάτεχε σαυτόν, καρτέρει.
οὐδὲν γὰρ ἀδικεῖ Μοσχίων σε. παράβολος
ὁ λόγος ἴσως ἐστ', ἄνδρες, ἀλλ' ἀληθινός.
εἰ μὲν γὰρ ἦ βουλόμενος ἢ κεκνισμένος   330
ἔρωτι τοῦτ' ἔπραξεν ἢ μισῶν ἐμέ,   (116)
ἦν ἂν ἐπὶ τῆς αὐτῆς διανοίας ἔτι θρασὺς
ἐμοί τε παρατεταγμένος. νυνὶ δέ μοι

and that Khrysis is rearing it now for Moskhion's sake.

PARMENON: Who says so?

DEMEAS: Everyone. But give me an answer. Is this true?

PARMENON: It is, master, but we wanted it not to become
known — 320

DEMEAS: What do you mean 'not to become known'?
[*He shouts inside to his slaves.*] Someone give me a rope
so that I can deal with this scoundrel.

PARMENON: No, I beg you.

DEMEAS: I'll brand you, I tell you.

PARMENON: Brand *me*?

DEMEAS: And soon.

PARMENON: I've had it. [*He takes to his heels and runs. At
this moment a slave with a rope appears and it is probably
he who is sent off at 325.*]

DEMEAS: Where are you going, you rogue, where? Catch
him!

O Citadel of Kekrops' land! O thin-spread aithēr! O — 325
[*He checks and brings himself back to earth.*]
Why are you shouting, Demeas? Why are you shouting, you
fool? Restrain yourself. Bear up! Moskhion has done you
no wrong. [*Turning to audience*] This a paradoxical thing
to say, gentlemen, but it's true. If he had done what he has 330
done willingly, or because of an infatuation or out of hatred
for me, he would still be brazening it out and opposing me.
As it is

41

ἀπολελόγηται τὸν φανέντ' αὑτῶι γάμον
ἄσμενος ἀκούσας. οὐκ ἐρῶν γάρ, ὡς ἐγὼ   335
τότ' ὠιόμην, ἔσπευδεν, ἀλλὰ τὴν ἐμὴν   (121)
Ἑλένην φυγεῖν βουλόμενος ἔνδοθέν ποτε·
αὕτη γάρ ἐστιν αἰτία τοῦ γεγονότος·
παρέλαβεν αὐτόν που μεθύοντα δηλαδή,
οὐκ ὄντ' ἐν ἑαυτοῦ· πολλὰ δ' ἐξεργάζεται   340
ἀνόητ' ἄκρατος καὶ νεότης, ὅταν λάβηι   (126)
τὸν συνεπιβουλεύσοντα τούτοις πλησίον.
οὐδενὶ τρόπωι γὰρ πιθανὸν εἶναί μοι δοκεῖ
τὸν εἰς ἅπαντας κόσμιον καὶ σώφρονα
τοὺς ἀλλοτρίους εἰς ἐμὲ τοιοῦτον γεγονέναι,   345
οὐδ' εἰ δεκάκις ποητός ἐστι, μὴ γόνωι   (131)
ἐμὸς ὑός· οὐ γὰρ τοῦτο, τὸν τρόπον δ' ὁρῶ.
χαμαιτύπη δ' ἄνθρωπος, ὄλεθρος. ἀλλὰ τί;
οὐ γὰρ περίεσται. Δημέα, νῦν ἄνδρα χρὴ
εἶναί σ'· ἐπιλαθοῦ τοῦ πόθου, πέπαυσ' ἐρῶν, 350
καὶ τἀτύχημα μὲν τὸ γεγονὸς κρύφθ' ὅσον   (136)
ἔνεστι διὰ τὸν ὑόν, ἐκ τῆς δ' οἰκίας
ἐπὶ κεφαλὴν ἐς κόρακας ὦσον τὴν καλὴν
Σαμίαν. ἔχεις δὲ πρόφασιν ὅτι τὸ παιδίον
ἀνεῖλετ'· ἐμφανίσηις γὰρ ἄλλο μηδὲ ἕν,   355
δακὼν δ' ἀνάσχου, καρτέρησον εὐγενῶς.   (141)

(Μα.) ἀλλ' ἆρα πρόσθε τῶν θυρῶν ἔστ' ἐνθάδε;
παῖ, Παρμένων. ἄνθρωπος ἀποδέδρακέ με,
ἀλλ' οὐδὲ μικρὸν συλλαβών.

342   συνεπιβουλεύσοντα z: συνεπιβουλευσαντα CB

he has cleared himself. He was glad to accept the marriage
once I suggested it. His readiness was not, as I thought then,   335
the product of love. He wants to get away from my house
and my Helen. She is responsible for what has happened.
Obviously she caught him when he had had a little too much
to drink, when he wasn't in control of himself. Strong wine   340
and youth collaborate to produce much folly when they
find an accomplice nearby. I simply cannot believe that
Moskhion who was so well-behaved and self-controlled in
dealings with others could behave in such a fashion towards
me, his father, not even if he is ten times my adopted son,   345
not my son by birth. It's not his origins I care about, it's
his character. The creature's a common whore, a pestilence!
But what of it? She won't prevail. Demeas, now you must
be a man. Forget your passion. Stop loving her! As far as   350
you can, keep the present misfortune dark. Do it for your
son's sake. Drive the fair Samian head-first from your house,   355
drive her to hell! You have an excuse. She kept the child.
Don't make anything else public. Bite your lip and bear it
like a man!

> [*At this inopportune moment the cook comes out of
> Demeas' house looking for Parmenon.*]

COOK: Surely he must be here, in front of the house?
Parmenon! [*When there is no answer, he soliloquizes.*] The
man's deserted me! He didn't help me the least bit.

Δη.   ἐκ τοῦ μέσου
ἄναγε σεαυτόν.

(Μα.)   Ἡράκλεις. τί τοῦτο, παῖ;   360
μαινόμενος εἰσδεδράμηκεν εἴσω τις γέρων˙   (146)
ἢ τί τὸ κακόν ποτ' ἐστί; τί δέ μοι τοῦτο, παῖ;
νὴ τὸν Ποσειδῶ, μαίνεθ', ὡς ἐμοὶ δοκεῖ˙
κέκραγε γοῦν παμμέγεθες. ἀστεῖον πάνυ
εἰ τὰς λοπάδας ἐν τῶι μέσωι μου κειμένας   365
ὄστρακα ποῆσαι πάνθ' ὅμοια. τὴν θύραν   (151)
πέπληχεν. ἐξώλης ἀπόλοιο, Παρμένων,
κομίσας με δεῦρο. μικρὸν ὑπαποστήσομαι.

(Δη.) οὔκουν ἀκούεις; ἄπιθι.

(Χρ.)   ποῖ γῆς, ὦ τάλαν;

(Δη.) ἐς κόρακας ἤδη.

(Χρ.)   δύσμορος.

(Δη.)   ναί, δύσμορος.   370
ἐλεινὸν ἀμέλει τὸ δάκρυον. παύσω σ' ἐγώ,   (156)
ὡς οἴομαι –

(Χρ.)   τί ποοῦσαν;

(Δη.)   οὐδέν. ἀλλ' ἔχεις
τὸ παιδίον, τὴν γραῦν˙ ἀποφθείρου ποτέ.

366   ποιήσοι παντ' ομοια˙ C: ποιησαι πανθ' ετοιμ[B
373   ποτε B: ταχυ C

44

[*Demeas rushes into the house,brushing the cook aside.*]

DEMEAS: Back! Out of my way!

COOK: Goodness! What's up? Some old madman has rushed
  into the house! What's the matter? It's nothing to do with   360
  me. He's mad: he looks that way to me. At any rate he
  shouted loud enough. Very nice indeed if he were to make
  potsherds of all the dishes that are on view. He's banged   365
  the door. Damn you, Parmenon, for bringing me here! I'll
  stand aside a little.

  [*He moves away from the door of Demeas' house.
  Khrysis is pushed on to the stage (either she is carrying
  her baby or an old woman comes with her carrying it):
  Demeas follows driving her out.*]

DEMEAS: Haven't you heard. Be off!

KHRYSIS: Where am I to go? Dear me!

DEMEAS: Get the hell out of here!

KHRYSIS: Poor me!

DEMEAS: Quite so, poor you! Your tears, so pitiable! I'll   370
  stop you, I can assure you.

KHRYSIS: Stop me doing what?

DEMEAS: Nothing. You've got the child, the old woman.
  To hell with you! Get you gone!

(Χρ.) ὅτι τοῦτ' ἀνειλόμην;

(Δη.)   διὰ τοῦτο καί -

(Χρ.)   τί "καί";

(Δη.) διὰ τοῦτο.

Μα.   τοιοῦτ' ἦν τὸ κακόν.

Χρ.   <οὐ> μανθάνω.   375

(Δη.) τρυφᾶν γὰρ οὐκ ἠπίστασο.

Χρ.   οὐκ ἠπιστάμην;   (161)
τί δ' ἐσθ'ὃ λέγεις;

(Δη.)   καίτοι πρὸς ἔμ᾿ ἦλθες ἐνθάδε
ἐν σινδονίτηι, Χρυσί - μανθάνεις: -πάνυ
λιτῶι.

(Χρ.)   τί οὖν;

(Δη.)   τότ' ἦν ἐγώ σοι πάνθ', ὅτε
φαύλως ἔπραττες.

(Χρ.)   νῦν δὲ τίς;

(Δη.)   μή μοι λάλει.   380
ἔχεις τὰ σαυτῆς πάντα· προστίθημί σοι   (166)
ἐγὼ θεραπαίνας, Χρυσί. ἐκ τῆς οἰκίας
ἄπιθι.

375   τοιουτ' ηντο C: [[μαγειρ]] τουτ' ηντιτο B

KHRYSIS: Just because I did not get rid of the baby?

DEMEAS: Because of this and —

KHRYSIS: And what?

COOK [*commenting aside*]: That's what the trouble is. I   375
understand now.

DEMEAS: You did not know how to live in luxury.

KHRYSIS: I did not know? What do you mean?

DEMEAS: You came here in a linen shift, Khrysis — you know
what I mean? — a plain one.

KHRYSIS: What of it?

DEMEAS: Then I was everything to you, when you were not
doing so well.

KHRYSIS: And now who is?

DEMEAS: Don't talk to me! You have all your possessions.
I give you as well servants, gold. Leave my house!   380

Μα.   τὸ πρᾶγμ' ὀργή τις ἐστί· προσιτέον.
βέλτισθ', ὅρα –

(Δη.)   τί μοι διαλέγει;

(Μα.)   μὴ δάκηις.

(Δη.) ἑτέρα γὰρ ἀγαπήσει τὰ παρ'ἐμοί, Χρυσί· νὴ   385
καὶ τοῖς θεοῖς θύσει.

Μα.   τί ἐστίν;

(Δη.)   ἀλλὰ σὺ
ὑὸν πεπόησαι· πάντ' ἔχεις.

(Μα.)   οὔπω δάκνει.
ὅμως –

(Δη.)   κατάξω τὴν κεφαλὴν ἄνθρωπέ σου
ἄν μοι διαλέγηι.

(Μα.)   νὴ δικαίως γ'· ἀλλ' ἰδού,
εἰσέρχομ' ἤδη.

(Δη.)   τὸ μέγα πρᾶγμ', ἐν τῆι πόλει   390
ὄψει σεαυτὴν νῦν ἀκριβῶς ἥτις εἶ.   (176)
οὐ κατά σε, Χρυσί, πραττόμεναι δραχμὰς δέκα

384   τιδημοι B
385   νη O^I: νυν BC
386   τι εστιν: αλλα συ C: τις εστιν: αλλα συ B   αλλα τι O^I
387   πεποηκας C   δακνει: O^I
389   νηδικαιωσγ' B: καιδικαιως C

48

COOK [*again commenting aside*]: It's some outburst of anger.
I'd better approach them.
  [*He attempts to address Demeas.*]
Sir, consider —
DEMEAS: Why are you talking to me?
COOK: Don't bite my head off! [*He retreats.*]
DEMEAS: [*turning to Khrysis*]: Another girl will be content
with what I have to offer, Khrysis, and will thank the gods
for it.   385
COOK [*aside*]: What does he mean?
DEMEAS: You've got a son. You have everything you want.
COOK [*aside*] He's not biting yet. [*He attempts once more
to address Demeas.*]
Even so —
DEMEAS [*threatening him with his stick*]: I'll smash your
head in if you talk to me.
COOK [*retreating*] You're quite right. Look! I'm off inside.
  [*He exits hurriedly into Demeas' house.*]
DEMEAS [*turning back to Khrysis*] Such an important   390
person! Once you are in town, you'll find out very well
who you are. Girls not on your level who earn just ten
drakhmai

μόνας ἕτεραι τρέχουσιν ἐπὶ τὰ δεῖπνα καὶ
πίνουσ' ἄκρατον ἄχρι ἂν ἀποθανῶσιν, ἢ
πεινῶσιν ἂν μὴ τοῦθ' ἑτοίμως καὶ ταχὺ   395
ποῶσιν. εἴσει δ' οὐδενὸς τοῦτ', οἶδ' ὅτι,   (181)
ἧττον σύ, καὶ γνώσει τίς οὖσ' ἡμάρτανες.
ἔσταθι.

(Χρ.)   τάλαιν' ἔγωγε τῆς ἐμῆς τύχης.

Νι.   τουτὶ τὸ πρόβατον τοῖς θεοῖς μὲν τὰ νόμιμα
ἅπαντα ποιήσει θυθὲν καὶ ταῖς θεαῖς.   400
αἷμα γὰρ ἔχει, χολὴν ἱκανήν, ὀστᾶ καλά,   (186)
σπλῆνα μέγαν, ὧν χρεία' στι τοῖς 'Ολυμπίοις
πέμψω δὲ γεύσασθαι κατακόψας τοῖς φίλοις
τὸ κωίδιον· λοιπὸν γάρ ἐστι τοῦτό μοι.
ἀλλ', 'Ηράκλεις, τί τοῦτο; πρόσθε τῶν θυρῶν 405
ἕστηκε Χρυσὶς ἥδε κλάους'; οὐ μὲν οὖν   (191)
ἄλλη. τί ποτε τὸ γεγονός;

(Χρ.)   ἐκβέβληκέ με
ὁ φίλος ὁ χρηστός σου. τί γὰρ ἄλλο;

(Νι.)   ὦ 'Ηράκλεις.
τίς; Δημέας;

(Χρ.)   ναί.

(Νι.)   διὰ τί;

(Χρ.)   διὰ τὸ παιδίον.

(Νι.) ἤκουσα καὐτὸς τῶν γυναικῶν ὅτι τρέφεις   410

run off to dinners and drink strong wine until they die or
else they go hungry if they don't do this readily and
quickly. You will get to know this, I'm sure, as well as any   395
of them and you will realise who you were and what a
mistake you made. Stay there!

    [*Exit Demeas.*]

KHRYSIS: Ah me! What misfortune!

    [*Nikeratos now enters returning from market with a
    sheep. He does not observe Khrysis.*]

NIKERATOS: Once it's sacrificed, this sheep will provide
everything expected for the gods and goddesses, It has   400
blood, an adequate gall-bladder, good bones, a big spleen,
everything the Olympians require. I'll chop up the skin
and send it to my friends to taste. That's all I'll have left.

    [*He turns and sees Khrysis.*]

Good heavens! What's this. Is this Khrysis I see standing in   405
front of the door, weeping? Indeed it is. [*addressing her*]
Whatever has happened?

KHRYSIS: Your fine friend has thrown me out. That's
what's happened.

NIKERATOS: Good heavens! Who has? Demeas?

KHRYSIS: Yes.

NIKERATOS: Why?

KHRYSIS: Because of the baby.

NIKERATOS: My womenfolk told me you had taken in the   410
baby and were rearing it.

ἀνελομένη παιδάριον. ἐμβροντησία.   (196)
ἀλλ' ἔστ' ἐκεῖνος ἡδύς.

<Χρ.>   οὐκ ὠργίζετο
εὐθύς, διαλιπὼν δ'.

<Νι.>   ἀρτίως;

<Χρ.>   ὃς καὶ φράσας
εἰς τοὺς γάμους μοι τἄνδον εὐτρεπῆ ποεῖν
μεταξύ μ' ὥσπερ ἐμμανὴς ἐπεισπεσὼν   415
ἔξωθεν ἐκκέκλεικε.

(Νι.)   Δημέας χολᾶι.   (201)
ὁ Πόντος οὐχ ὑγιεινόν ἐστι χωρίον.
πρὸς τὴν γυναῖκα δεῦρ' ἀκολούθει τὴν ἐμήν.
θάρρει· τί βούλει; παύσεθ' οὗτος ἀπομανεὶς
ὅταν λογισμὸν ὧν ποεῖ νυνὶ λάβηι.   420

                    ΧΟΡΟΥ

Lunacy! Still he's an easy going fellow.

KHRYSIS: He didn't become angry at the start, but after an interval.

NIKERATOS: Just now?

KHRYSIS: Yes, the very one who, after telling me to get everything ready for the wedding, has rushed in like a madman and shut me out of his house.   415

NIKERATOS: Demeas can't be well. The Pontos is not a healthy place. Come with me to my wife. Cheer up. Why worry? He will recover from his madness when he thinks over what he is doing.

[*They all go into his house.*]   420

THE THIRD CHORAL INTERLUDE

ΜΕΡΟΣ Δ

ΝΙΚΗΡΑΤΟΣ
     παρατενεῖς, γύναι. βαδίζω νῦν ἐκείνωι
       προσβαλῶν.
     οὐδ' ἂν ἐπὶ πολλῶι γενέσθαι τὸ γεγονός, μὰ
       τοὺς θεούς,
     πρᾶγμ' ἐδεξάμην. μεταξὺ τῶν γάμων ποουμένων
     συμβέβηκ' οἰωνὸς ἡμῖν ἄτοπος· ἐκβεβλημένη
     εἰσελήλυθεν πρὸς ἡμᾶς παιδάριον ἔχουσά τις· 425
     δάκρυα γίνεθ', αἱ γυναῖκες τεθορύβηνται.
      Δημέας
     σκατοφαγεῖ. νὴ τὸν Ποσειδῶ καὶ θεούς, οἰμώξεται
     σκαιὸς ὤν.

Μο.   οὐ μὴ δύηι ποθ' Ἥλιος. τί δεῖ
     λέγειν;
     ἐπιλέλησθ' ἡ νὺξ ἑαυτῆς. ὦ μακρᾶς δείλης.
     τρίτον
     λούσομ' ἐλθών· τί γὰρ ἔχοιμ' ἂν ἄλλο ποιεῖν;

Νι.   Μοσχίων,   430
     χαῖρε πολλά.

(Μο.)   νῦν ποοῦμεν τοὺς γάμους; ὁ
       Παρμένων
     εἶπεν ἐν ἀγοραῖ περιτυχὼν ἄρτι μοι. τί κωλύει
     μετιέναι τὴν παῖδά μ' ἤδη;

(Νι.)   τἀνθάδ' ἀγνοῶν πάρει;

(Μο.) ποῖα;

ACT FOUR

[*Nikeratos enters speaking back into his house and completing a conversation with his wife.*]

NIKERATOS:

    You'll finish me off, wife. I'm just going to approach him.
    [*He soliloquizes*] I wouldn't have wanted to see this happen
    even if I'd been paid a lot of money. No, not at all. In the
    middle of the wedding we've come upon an untimely omen.
    A girl's been thrown out and come into my house with a   425
    baby. There's weeping. The women are in confusion.
    Demeas is behaving without any sensitivity. My word, he'll
    pay for his stupidity.

        [*Moskhion comes down one of the side-entrances solilo-*
        quizing and not noticing Nikeratos.]

MOSKHION: Won't the sun ever set? The only explanation
    is that night has forgot herself. What a long afternoon! I'll
    go and take my third bath. What else can I do?

NIKERATOS [*calling to Moskhion*]: Moskhion, I'm glad to   430
    see you.

MOSKHION: Are we starting the wedding now? Parmenon
    told me when he met me in the market a little while ago.
    Is there anything to stop me from going to fetch your
    daughter now?

NIKERATOS: You don't know what's happened since you
    left?

MOSKHION: What kind of thing?

(Νι.)   ποῖ'; ἀηδία τις συμβέβηκεν ἔκτοπος.

(Μο.)ʿΗράκλεις· τίς; οὐ γὰρ εἰδὼς ἔρχομαι.

(Νι.)   τὴν Χρυσίδα   435
     ἐξελήλακ' ἔνδοθέν σου, φίλταθ', ὁ πατὴρ ἀρτίως.

(Μο.) οἶον εἴρηκας.

(Νι.)   τὸ γεγονός.

(Μο.)   διὰ τί;

(Νι.)   διὰ τὸ παιδίον.

(Μο.) εἶτα ποῦ' στι νῦν;

(Νι.)   παρ' ἡμῖν ἔνδον.

(Μο.)   ὦ δεινὸν
     λέγων
   πρᾶγμα καὶ θαυμαστόν.

(Νι.)   εἴ σοι δεινὸν εἶναι
     φαίνεται –

Δη. ἂν λάβω ξύλον, ποήσω τὰ δάκρυ' ὑμῶν ταῦτ' ἐγὼ
                                                     440
     ἐκκεκόφθαι. τίς ὁ φλύαρος; οὐ διακονήσετε
     τῶι μαγείρωι; πάνυ γάρ ἐστιν ἄξιον, νὴ τὸν Δία,
     ἐπιδακρῦσαι· μέγα γὰρ ὑμῖν ὤιχετ' ἐκ τῆς
     οἰκίας

434   ποια: ποια φηις Β

56

NIKERATOS: What kind of thing? Something strange and
  unpleasant.
MOSKHION: Dear me! What exactly? I've arrived quite
  unaware of it.
NIKERATOS: Your father, dear boy, has just driven Khrysis   435
  out of his house..
MOSKHION: This can't be true.
NIKERATOS: It is.
MOSKHION: But why has he done this?
NIKERATOS: Because of the baby.
MOSKHION: Where is Khrysis now?
NIKERATOS: Inside, with us.
MOSKHION: What a strange and dreadful story!
NIKERATOS: If you really think it dreadful — [*Before
  Nikeratos can finish, Demeas suddenly emerges from his
  house speaking back into it. He does not see Nikeratos and
  Moskhion who converse sotto voce while he soliloquizes.*]
DEMEAS: If I get a stick, I'll beat these tears out of your   440
  eyes. What nonsense is this? Start giving the cook some
  help! It's a suitable occasion for tears of course! The house
  has suffered a great loss!

ἀγαθόν· αὐτὰ τἄργα δηλοῖ. χαῖρ', Ἄπολλον
    φίλτατε,
ἐπ' ἀγαθῆι τύχηι τε πᾶσι τοὺς γάμους <οὓς>
    μέλλομεν   445
<νῦν> ποεῖν ἡμῖν γενέσθαι δὸς σύ· μέλλω γὰρ
    ποεῖν
τοὺς γάμους, ἄνδρες, καταπιὼν τὴν χολήν· τήρ[ει
    δὲ σύ,
δέσποτ', αὐτὸς ἵνα γένωμαι μὴ' πίδηλος μηδ[ενί,
ἀλλὰ τὸν ὑμέναιον αἴδειν εἰσανάγκασόν με σύ.
        ο]ὐκ ἄριστ' ἐγὼ <‿> ὡς ἔχω νῦν. ἀλλὰ
    τί;   450
        ]νέλθοι.

(Νι.)   σὺ πρότερος, Μοσχίων,
    πρόσελθέ μου.

(Μο.) εἶεν· ὦ π]άτερ, τί ποιεῖς ταῦτα;

(Δη.)   ποῖα, Μοσχίων;

(Μο.) ποῖ', ἐρωτ]αῖς; διὰ τί Χρυσὶς οἴχετ' ἀπιοῦσ',
    εἰπέ μοι.

(Δη.) ......] πρεσβεύεταί τις πρός με· δεινόν. –
    οὐχὶ σόν,
μὰ τὸν Ἀπόλλω, τοὔργον ἐστίν ἀλλὰ παντελ[ῶς
    ἐμόν·   455
τίς ὁ φλύ]αρος; –δεινὸν ἤδη· συναδικεῖ μ' οὗτος

454   με z: εμε Β

58

The facts make this clear.

> [*He turns to the statue in front of his house-door (see the note on 444).*]

Dear Apollo! I greet you. Allow me to succeed in bringing
about the marriage we intend to make and may all be well.   445

> [*He turns to the audience.*]

I really do intend to accomplish the marriage, gentlemen,
and to swallow my anger.

> [*He turns back to the statue.*]

Make sure, Lord, that no one gets to know what I'm doing.
Force me instead to sing the wedding-hymn . . . best . . . as
I am . . . what of it?   450
?She'll never] come back

> [*The conversation between Nikeratos and Moskhion becomes audible once more.*]

NIKERATOS: You approach him first, Moskhion.

MOSKHION: All right — [*He goes over and confronts Demeas.*]
Father, why are you doing this?

DEMEAS: Doing what, Moskhion?

MOSKHION: You ask what? Why has Khrysis gone and left
us? Tell me!

DEMEAS: [*aside*]: Someone is sending ambassadors to me.
This is dreadful! [*To Moskhion*] It's not your affair. It's
my business entirely. What is this nonsense? [*Aside once*   455
more] This is quite dreadful. He too is wronging me.

(Μο.)   [τί φῄς;

(Δη.) περιφα]νῶς· τί γὰρ προσέρχεθ' ὑπὲρ ἐκείνης;
        ἀσ[μένωι
      χρῆν γὰρ αὐτῶι τοῦτο δήπου γε[γονέναι.

[Μο.]   τί τ]οὺς
        φίλους
      προσδοκαῖς ἐρεῖν πυθομένους;

(Δη.)   π[ροσδο]κῶ, Μοσχίων,
      τοὺς φίλους - ἔα με.

(Μο.)   ἀγεννὲς ἂν ποιοίην ἐπι-
        τρέπων.   460

(Δη.) ἀλλὰ κωλύσεις με;

(Μο.)   ἔγωγε.

(Δη.)   τοῦθ', ὁρᾶ[θ', ὑ]περβολή·
      τοῦτο τῶν δεινῶν ἐκείνων δεινότερον.

(Μο.)   οὐ πάντα
        γὰρ
      ἐπιτρέπειν ὀργῆι προσήκει.

Νι.   Δημέα, καλῶς λέγει.

Μο.   ἀποτρέχειν αὐτῆι φράσον δεῦρ' εἰσιών,
        Νικήρατε.

(Δη.) Μοσχίων, ἔα μ', ἔα με, Μοσχίων· τρίτον λέγω   465

MOSKHION: What are you saying?

DEMEAS [*continuing his reflections aside*]: It's quite clear.
Otherwise why does he approach me on her behalf? He
ought to have rejoiced over what has happened.

MOSKHION: What do you think our friends will say when
they find out?

DEMEAS [*at last addressing Moskhion*]: (I expect they'll —)
[*He breaks off and makes a direct appeal*] Let me go on.

MOSKHION: I would be acting despicably if I did.   460

DEMEAS: You'll try to stop me?

MOSKHION: I will.

DEMEAS [*probably to audience (see the note on 461)*]: You
see? This is the limit! This is worse than the other things.

MOSKHION: It's wrong to give everything over to anger.

NIKERATOS [*coming up and joining in the conversation*]:
He's right, you know, Demeas.

MOSKHION [*to Nikeratos*]: Go in and tell her to hurry up
and come back to our house, Nikeratos.

DEMEAS: Moskhion, let me, let me, Moskhion. I say this for
the third time.   465

τουτογί˙ πάντ' οἶδα.

(Μο.)   ποῖα πάντα;

(Δη.)   μή μοι διαλέγου.

(Μο.) ἀλλ' ἀνάγκη, πάτερ.

(Δη.)   ἀνάγκη; τῶν ἐμῶν οὐ κύριος
ἔσομ' ἐγώ;

(Μο.)   ταύτην ἐμοὶ δὸς τὴν χάριν.

(Δη.)   ποίαν
     χάριν;
οἷον ἀξιοῖς μ' ἀπελθεῖν αὐτὸν ἐκ τῆς οἰκίας
καταλιπόνθ' ὑμᾶς δύ' ὄντας. τοὺς γάμους ἔα
     ποεῖν,   470
τοὺς γάμους ἔα με ποιεῖν, ἂν ἔχῃς νοῦν.

(Μο.)   ἀλλ' ἐῶ˙
βούλομαι δὲ συμπαρεῖναι Χρυσίδ' ἡμῖν.

(Δη.)   Χρυσίδα;

(Μο.) ἕνεκα σοῦ σπεύδω μάλιστα τοῦτο.

(Δη.)   ταῦτ' οὐ γνώριμα,
οὐ σαφῆ; μαρτύρομαί σε, Λοξία, συνόμνυται
τοῖς ἐμοῖς ἐχθροῖς τις. οἴμοι˙ καὶ
     διαρραγήσομαι.   475

466   τουτογί z: τουτογε B

62

I know everything.

MOSKHION: What do you mean 'everything'?

DEMEAS: Don't talk to me!

MOSKHION: I must, father.

DEMEAS: You must? Am I not the master of my own household?

MOSKHION: Grant me one favour.

DEMEAS: What do you mean 'favour'? You're asking me, I suppose, to abandon my house and leave the two of you together. Let me carry out the wedding. You will if you have any sense. 470

MOSKHION: Go ahead. But Khrysis must be there with us.

DEMEAS: Khrysis?

MOSKHION: It's for your sake most of all I want this.

DEMEAS [*turning aside*]: Isn't it obvious? Isn't it clear? [*turning once more to the statue*] I call you as witness, 475
Apollo. Someone is conspiring with my enemies. Ah me! I shall burst!

(Μο.) τί δὲ λέγεις;

(Δη.)   βούλει φράσω σοι;

(Μο.)   πάνυ γε.

(Δη.)   δεῦρο δή.

(Μο.)   λέγε.

(Δη.) ἀλλ' ἐγώ. τὸ παιδίον σόν ἐστιν, οἶδ', ἀκήκοα
     τοῦ συνειδότος τὰ κρυπτὰ Παρμένοντος· ὥστε μὴ
     πρὸς ἐμὲ παῖζε.

(Μο.)   ἔπειτά σ' ἀδικεῖ Χρυσίς, εἰ
     τοῦτ' ἔστ' ἐμόν;

(Δη.) ἀλλα τίς; σύ;

(Μο.)   τί γὰρ ἐκείνη γέγονεν αἰτία;

(Δη.)   τί φῄς;   480
     οὐδὲν ἐνθυμεῖσθε;

(Μο.)   τί βοᾷς;

(Δη.)   ὅ τι βοῶ, κάθαρμα σύ;
     τοῦτ' ἐρωτᾷς; εἰς σεαυτὸν ἀναδέχει τὴν
        αἰτίαν,
     εἰπέ μοι; καὶ τοῦτο τολμᾷς ἐμβλέπων ἐμοὶ
        λέγειν;

478 ὥστε μὴ z: ωστεμηκετι Β   481   ουδεν: ουδεν Β
482-3 ειπεμοιεισεαυτοναναδέχειτηναιτιαν Β
          σ

64

MOSKHION: What are you saying?

DEMEAS: Do you want me to tell you?

MOSKHION: Yes, I do.

DEMEAS [*withdrawing a little to distance himself from Nikeratos, summons Moskhion*] This way.

MOSKHION [*following him*]: Tell me.

DEMEAS: I will. The child is yours. I know. I've heard from one who knows the secret, Parmenon. Stop playing games with me.

MOSKHION: In that case is *Khrysis* doing you wrong, if the child is *mine*?

DEMEAS: Who is then? You?

MOSKHION [*continuing his previous utterance*]: In what way is she to blame? 480

DEMEAS: What are you saying? Have you and Khrysis no conscience?

MOSKHION: Why are you shouting?

DEMEAS: Why am I shouting? You ask this, you scum! Tell me, do you take the blame upon yourself? Do you dare to look me in the face and say this?

παντελῶς οὕτως ἀπεγνωκώς με τυγχάνεις;

(Μο.)   ἐγώ;
διὰ τί;

(Δη.)   "διὰ τί" φῄς; ἐρωτᾶν δ' ἀξιοῖς;

(Μο.)   τὸ πρᾶγμα γὰρ
ἐστὶν οὐ πάνδεινον. ἀλλὰ μυρίοι δήπου, πάτερ,
                                              486
τοῦτο πεποήκασιν.

(Δη.)   ὦ Ζεῦ, τοῦ θράσους. ἐναντίον
δή σ' ἐρωτῶ τῶν παρόντων· ἐκ τίνος τὸ παιδίον
ἐστί σοι; Νικηράτωι τοῦτ' εἶπον, εἰ μή σοι
    δοκεῖ
δεινὸν <εἶναι.>

(Μο.)   νὴ Δί', ἀλλὰ δεινὸν οὕτω γίγνεται
                                              490
τοῦτο πρὸς τοῦτον λέγειν με· χαλεπανεῖ γὰρ
    πυθόμενος.

Νι. ὦ κάκιστ' ἀνδρῶν ἀπάντων· ὑπονοεῖν γὰρ ἄρχομαι
τὴν τύχην καὶ τἀσέβημα τὸ γεγονὸς μόλις ποτέ.

Μο. τέλος ἔχω τοίνυν ἐγώ.

Δη.   νῦν αἰσθάνει, Νικήρατε;

(Νι.) οὐ γάρ; ὦ πάνδεινον ἔργον· ὦ τὰ Τηρέως λέχη 495
Οἰδίπου τε καὶ Θυέστου καὶ τὰ τῶν ἄλλων, ὅσα
γεγονόθ' ἡμῖν ἐστ' ἀκοῦσαι, μικρὰ ποιήσας –

Is your rejection of me so complete?

MOSKHION: Me? Why?

DEMEAS: 'Why' you say? You really need to ask?

MOSKHION: It's not so dreadful. Thousands, I believe have
  done this sort of thing, father.   485

DEMEAS: My god! What effrontery! I ask you before witnesses. Who is the mother of the child? Tell Nikeratos if
  you don't think it's so dreadful.

MOSKHION: Yes, but if I tell him this just like that I make
  it dreadful. Once he finds out he will be angry.   490

  [*Nikeratos, at last aware of what is going on, bursts into
  the conversation.*]

NIKERATOS: O worst of all men! At last I begin to realise
  what has happened and what an outrageous crime has been
  perpetrated!

MOSKHION: This is the end of me.

DEMEAS: You realise now, Nikeratos?

NIKERATOS: Of course. O deed most dreadful! O thou who
  makes insignificant the bed of Tereus or Oidipous or   495
  Thyestes or of any of the others we have come to know
  about —

(Μο.)   ἐγώ;

(Νι.) τοῦτ' ἐτόλμησας σὺ πρᾶξαι, τοῦτ' ἔτλης;
           Ἀμύντορος
        νῦν ἐχρῆν ὀργὴν λαβεῖν σε, Δημέα, καὶ τουτονὶ
        ἐκτυφλῶσαι.

(Δη.)   διά σε τούτωι γέγονε πάντα καταφανῆ.
                                                              500

(Νι.) τίνος ἀπόσχοι' ἂν σύ; ποῖον οὐκ ἂν[
        εἶτ' ἐγώ σοι δῶ γυναῖκα τὴν ἐμαυτ[οῦ θυγατέρα;
        πρότερον – εἰς κόλπον δέ φασι· τὴν Ἀδ[ράστειαν
           σέβω –
        ἐπὶ Διομνήστωι γενοίμην νυμφίωι[
        ὁμολογουμένην ἀτυχίαν.

(Δη.)   τα.[505
        ἠδικημένος κατεῖχον.

(Νι.)   ἀνδράποδ[ον εἶ, Δημέα.
        εἰ γὰρ ἠῖ[σχυνε λέ]κτρον, οὐκ ἂν εἰς ἄλλον ποτὲ
        ὕβρισ' οὐδ' ἡ συγ[κλ]ιθεῖσα· παλλακὴν δ'ἂν
           αὔριον
        πρῶτος ἀνθρώπων ἐπώλουν, συναποκηρύττων ἅμα
        υἱόν, ὥστε μηδὲν εἶναι μήτε κουρεῖον κενόν,   510
        μὴ στοάν, καθημένους δὲ πάντας ἐξ ἑωθινοῦ
        περὶ ἐμοῦ λαλεῖν λέγοντας ὡς ἀνὴρ Νικήρατος
        γέγον' ἐπεξελθὼν δικαίως τῶι φόνωι.

(Μο.)   ποίωι φόνωι;

68

MOSKHION: You mean me?

NIKERATOS: You dared to do this, you durst do this?
Demeas, you must assume the anger of Amyntor and blind
this man.

DEMEAS [*to Moskhion*]: It's your fault he's got to know of
this.   500

NIKERATOS [*continuing his assault of Moskhion*]: What
would you keep your hands off? What would you not . . .
Am I to give my daughter to you? I'd rather — into one's
lap, as they say; for I revere Adrasteia. I'd rather be father-
in-law to Diomnestos . . . bad luck everyone acknowledges.   505

DEMEAS: . . . wronged I was holding . . .

NIKERATOS: You're no better than a slave, Demeas. If he
had sullied my couch, he would have wronged no other man
nor would his bedmate. My concubine I'd have sold to-
morrow and disowned my son at the same time. Everyone
would have known. No barber's shop, no colonnade would   510
have been empty. Everyone would have sat from morning
on talking about me and saying that Nikeratos was a real
man, because he did the right thing and prosecuted his son
for murder.

MOSKHION: What murder?

(Νι.) φόνον ἐγὼ κρίνω τὰ τοιαῦθ' ὅστις ἐπαναστὰς
     ποεῖ.

Μο. αὖός εἰμι καὶ πέπηγα τῶι κακῶι, νὴ τοὺς θεούς.

                                                      515

(Νι.) ἀλλ' ἐγὼ πρὸς τοῖσιν ἄλλοις τὴν τὰ δείν'
     εἰργασμένην
     εἰσεδεξάμην μελάθροις τοῖς ἐμοῖς.

(Δη.)   Νικήρατε,
     ἔκβαλ', ἱκετεύω· συναδικοῦ γνησίως ὡς ἂν φίλος.

(Νι.) ὃς διαρραγήσομ' <ἐπι>δών. ἐμβλέπεις μοι,
     βάρβαρε,
     Θρᾶιξ ἀληθῶς; οὔ παρήσεις;

Μο.   πάτερ ἄκουσον, πρὸς
     θεῶν.   520

(Δη.) οὐκ ἀκούσομ' οὐθέν.

(Μο.)   οὐδ' εἰ μηδὲν ὧν σὺ
     προσδοκᾷς
     γέγονεν; ἄρτι γὰρ τὸ πρᾶγμα κατανοῶ.

(Δη.)   πῶς μηδὲ ἕν;

(Μο.) οὐχὶ Χρυσίς ἐστι μήτηρ οὗ τρέφει νῦν παιδίον,
     ἀλλ' ἐμοὶ χαρίζεται τοῦθ' ὁμολογοῦσ' αὐτῆς.

521   οὐδ' εἰ μηδὲν z: νηδιουδεν B

NIKERATOS: I consider it murder when someone attacks me
and does such things.

MOSKHION: I'm dried up and frozen by all this. 515

NIKERATOS: On top of everything, I've received into my
halls the perpetrator of these horrors, Khrysis.

DEMEAS: Nikeratos, I beg you, throw her out. Share in my
discomfort, nobly as a friend would.

NIKERATOS: Of course; I'll split down the middle just at the
sight of her. [*to Moskhion*] You look me in the face?
You're no Greek, a true Thracian. Let me past. [*He rushes* 520
into his house.]

MOSKHION: Listen father, I beg you.

DEMEAS: I'll listen to nothing.

MOSKHION: Even if nothing of what you suspect has
occurred? I know now what has happened.

DEMEAS: What do you mean 'nothing'?

MOSKHION: Khrysis is not the mother of the child she is
rearing. She is doing this as a favour, pretending it's her
child.

τί φῄς;

(Μο.) τὰς ἀληθείας.

(Δη.)   διὰ τί δὲ τοῦτό σοι χαρίζεται; 525

(Μο.) οὐχ ἑκὼν λέγω μέν, ἀλλὰ μείζον' αἰτίαν φυγὼν
λαμβάνω μικράν, ἐὰν σὺ τὸ γεγονὸς πύθηι σαφῶς.

(Δη.) ἀλλ' ἀποκτενεῖς πρὶν εἰπεῖν.

(Μο.)   ἔστι τῆς Νικηράτου
θυγατρός, ἐξ ἐμοῦ. λαθεῖν δὲ τοῦτ' ἐβουλόμην
ἐγώ.

(Δη.) πῶς λέγεις;

(Μο.)   ὥσπερ πέπρακται.

(Δη.)   μή με βουκολεῖς ὅρα.   530

(Μο.) οὐ λαβεῖν ἔλεγχόν ἐστι; καὶ τί κερδανῶ πλέον;

(Δη.) οὐθέν. ἀλλὰ τὴν θύραν τις –

Νι.   ὦ τάλας ἐγώ, τάλας·
οἷον εἰσιδὼν θέαμα διὰ θυρῶν ἐπείγομαι
ἐμμανὴς ἀπροσδοκήτωι καρδίαν πληγεὶς ἄχει.

Δη. τί ποτ' ἐρεῖ;

(Νι.)   τὴν θυγατέρ' <ἄρτι> τὴν ἐμὴν τῶι
παιδίωι
τιτθίον διδοῦσαν ἔνδον κατέλαβον.

72

DEMEAS: Really?

MOSKHION: It's true.

DEMEAS: Why is she doing this favour for you?   525

MOSKHION: I don't want to reveal this, but if you get to
know the truth I shall avoid the greater blame and accept
the lesser.

DEMEAS: You'll be the death of me if you don't say what
you mean.

MOSKHION: The mother of the baby is Nikeratos' daughter
and I am the father. I wanted to keep this from you.

DEMEAS: What are you saying?

MOSKHION: Exactly what happened.   530

DEMEAS: Take care: don't try to cheat me.

MOSKHION: Where proof is at hand? And what would I
gain?

DEMEAS: Nothing. But the door —

[*Nikeratos bursts on to the stage from his house.*]

NIKERATOS: Ah me! Ah me! What a sight I have seen! I
sped through the door, maddened, pierced to the heart with
unexpected woe!

DEMEAS: Whatever will he say?

NIKERATOS: I came upon my daughter just now feeding her
baby.   535

(Δη.)   τοῦτ' ἦν ἄρα.   536

Μο.   πάτερ, ἀκούεις;

(Δη.)   οὐδὲν ἀδικεῖς Μοσχίων <μ'>· ἐγὼ
        δέ σε
    ὑπονοῶν τοιαῦτα.

(Νι.)   πρός σε, Δημέα, πορεύομαι.

Μο.   ἐκποδὼν ἄπειμι.

(Δη.)   θάρρει.

(Μο.)   τουτονὶ τέθνηχ' ὁρῶν.

(Δη.) τί τὸ πάθος δ' ἐστίν;

Νι.   διδοῦσαν τιτθίον τῶι παιδίωι
    ἀρτίως ἔνδον κατέλαβον τὴν ἐμαυτοῦ θυγατέρα.
                                             541

(Δη.) τυχὸν ἔπαιζεν.

(Νι.)   οὐκ ἔπαιζεν. ὡς γὰρ εἰσιόντα με
    εἶδεν, ἐξαίφνης κατέπεσεν.

(Δη.)   τυχὸν ἴσως ἔδοξε [γάρ-

(Νι.) παρατενεῖς "τυχὸν" λέγων μοι πάντα.

(Δη.)   (τούτων αἴτιος
    εἴμ' ἐγώ.)

74

DEMEAS: So it's true.

MOSKHION: You hear this, father?

DEMEAS: It's not you that is in the wrong, but I am, for suspecting you.

NIKERATOS: Demeas, I'm coming to you.

MOSKHION: I'm off.

DEMEAS: Courage.

MOSKHION: When I look at him, I die.

[*Moskhion leaves by one of the side-entrances.*]

DEMEAS: What's wrong?

NIKERATOS: Just now I came upon my daughter offering   540
her breast to the baby.

DEMEAS: Perhaps she was just playing.

NIKERATOS: She certainly wasn't. As soon as she saw me,
she fainted.

DEMEAS: Perhaps she thought —

NIKERATOS: You'll kill me with all your 'perhapses'.

DEMEAS: [*aside*]: This is all my fault.

(Νι.)   τί φῄς;

(Δη.)   ἄπιστον πρᾶγμά μοι δοκεῖς
   λέγειν.   545

(Νι.) ἀλλὰ μὴν εἶδον.

(Δη.)   κορυζαῖς.

(Νι.)   οὗτος οὐκ ἔστιν λόγος.
   ἀλλὰ πάλιν ἐλθών –

(Δη.)   τὸ δεῖνα· μικρόν, ὦ τᾶν –οἴχεται.
   πάντα πράγματ' ἀνατέτραπται, τέλος ἔχει. νὴ
      τὸν Δία,
   οὑτοσὶ τὸ πρᾶγμ' ἀκούσας χαλεπανεῖ, κεκράξεται·
                                                 549
   τραχὺς ἄνθρωπος σκατοφάγος, αὐθέκαστος τῶι
      τρόπωι.
   ἐμὲ γὰρ ὑπονοεῖν τοιαῦτα τὸν μιαρὸν ἐχρῆν, ἐμέ;
                                                 (206)
   νὴ τὸν ῞Ηφαιστον δικαίως ἀποθάνοιμ' ἄν.
      ῾Ηράκλεις,
   ἡλίκον κέκραγε. τοῦτ' ἦν· πῦρ βοᾷ· τὸ παιδίον
   φησὶν ἐμπρήσειν ἀπειλῶν. υἱδοῦν ὀπτώμενον
   ὄψομαι. πάλιν πέπληχε τὴν θύραν. στρόβιλος ἢ
                                                 555
   σκηπτὸς ἄνθρωπός τις ἐστί.

Νι.   Δημέα, συνίσταται   (211)

547   ωταλαν Β

NIKERATOS: What are you saying?

DEMEAS: I can't believe what you say. 545

NIKERATOS: I've seen it.

DEMEAS: You're talking drivel.

NIKERATOS: This is no mere story. I'd better go back in.
[*He rushes into his house.*]

DEMEAS: You know — wait a moment, my dear fellow. He's
gone. Everything is in confusion. It's all up. Once this man
gets to know the truth he will be angry, he'll shout his head
off. He is rough, insensitive, independent in character. Was
I the one who had to harbour such suspicions, **damn** me,
was I! [*There is an off-stage noise coming from Nikeratos'* 550
house.] This is it. He calls for fire. He threatens to burn
the baby. I'll see my grandson roasted. He's banged the
door again. The man's a whirlwind or a thunderbolt. 555
[*Nikeratos enters.*]

NIKERATOS: Demeas, Khrysis is conspiring

　　　　ἐπ' ἐμὲ καὶ πάνδεινα ποιεῖ πράγμαθ' ἡ Χρυσίς.

(Δη.)　　　　　　　　　　　　　　　　　　　　τί φῄς;

(Νι.)　τὴν γυναῖκά μου πέπεικε μηθὲν ὁμολογεῖν ὅλως
　　　μηδὲ τὴν κόρην, ἔχει δὲ πρὸς βίαν τὸ παιδίον
　　　οὐ προήσεσθαί τε φησίν· ὥστε μὴ θαύμαζ', ἐὰν
　　　　　　　　　　　　　　　　　　　　　　　　　560
　　　αὐτόχειρ αὐτῆς γένωμαι.

Δη.　　　　　　　　τῆς γυναικὸς αὐτόχειρ;　　　(216)

(Νι.)　πάντα γὰρ σύνοιδεν αὕτη.

(Δη.)　　　　　　　　　　　　μηδαμῶς, Νικήρατε.

(Νι.)　σοὶ δ' ἐβουλόμην προειπεῖν.

(Δη.)　　　　　　　　　　　　　οὑτοσὶ μελαγχολᾷ.
　　　εἰσπεπήδηκεν. τί τούτοις τοῖς κακοῖς τις
　　　　χρήσεται;
　　　οὐδεπώποτ' εἰς τοιαύτην ἐμπεσών, μὰ τοὺς
　　　　θεούς,　　　　　　　　　　　　　　　　565
　　　οἶδα ταραχήν. ἔστι μέντοι τὸ γεγονὸς φράσαι
　　　　σαφῶς　　　　　　　　　　　　　　　　(221)
　　　πολὺ κράτιστον. ἀλλ', Ἄπολλον, ἡ θύρα πάλιν
　　　　ψοφεῖ.

Χρ.　ὦ τάλαιν' ἐγώ, τί δράσω; ποῖ φύγω; τὸ παιδίον
　　　λήψεταί μου.

Δη.　　　　　Χρυσί, δεῦρο.

against me and doing the most dreadful things.

DEMEAS: What do you mean?

NIKERATOS: She's persuaded my wife and daughter to admit
nothing and she's grabbed hold of the baby and won't
release it. Don't be surprised if I kill her.   560

DEMEAS: Kill your wife?

NIKERATOS: She's in the plot.

DEMEAS: Don't, Nikeratos.

NIKERATOS: I wanted to give you advance warning. [*He
goes back into his house.*]

DEMEAS: He's mad. He's rushed inside. How is one to deal
with this? I've never been in such a mêlée. The best thing   565
to do is to explain clearly what has happened. Apollo! I
hear the door again. [*Khrysis rushes out of Nikeratos'
house, carrying the baby.*]

KHRYSIS: Ah me! What am I to do? Where am I to flee?
He'll take my baby.

DEMEAS: Here, Khrysis.

(Χρ.)   τίς καλεῖ με;

(Δη.)   εἴσω τρέχε.

Νι. ποῖ σύ, ποῖ φεύγεις;

(Δη.)   Ἄπολλον, μονομαχήσω τήμερον, 570
ὡς ἔοικ', ἐγώ. τί βούλει; τίνα διώκεις;

(Νι.)   Δημέα,   (226)
ἐκποδὼν ἄπελθ'· ἔα με γενόμενον τοῦ παιδίου

·   ἐγκρατῆ τὸ πρᾶγμ' ἀκοῦσαι τῶν γυναικῶν.

(Δη.)   μηθαμῶς.

(Νι.) ἀλλὰ τυπτήσεις με:

(Δη.)   ἔγωγε. – θᾶττον εἰσφθάρηθι σύ.

(Νι.) ἀλλὰ μὴν κἀγώ σε.

(Δη.)   φεῦγε Χρυσί· κρείττων ἐστί μου. 575

(Νι.) πρότερος ἅπτει μου σὺ νυνί· ταῦτ' ἐγὼ
μαρτύρομαι.   (231)

Δη. σὺ δ' ἐπ' ἐλευθέραν γυναῖκα λαμβάνεις βακτηρίαν
καὶ διώκεις.

(Νι.)   συκοφαντεῖς.

          η θαμως
573   μαινομαι   Β

KHRYSIS: Who calls me? [*She turns and sees Demeas.*]

DEMEAS: Run inside.

[*Nikeratos arrives in hot pursuit.*]

NIKERATOS: You there, where are you off to?

DEMEAS: Apollo, I'll have to fight today in single combat,   570
so it seems. [*To Nikeratos*] What do you want? Who are
you after?

NIKERATOS: Out of the way, Demeas. Let me get hold of
the child and hear what the women have to say.

DEMEAS: [*standing in his way*]: No!

NIKERATOS: You're going to hit me?

DEMEAS: Yes. [*To Khrysis*] Get the hell in there!

[*The two men grapple.*]

NIKERATOS: I'll strike you.

DEMEAS: Run, Khrysis! He's stronger than me.   575

[*Demeas manages to delay Nikeratos till Khrysis has
reached the safety of Demeas' house.*]

NIKERATOS: You began this. I call witnesses to this effect.

DEMEAS: *You* are taking a stick to a free woman and
pursuing her.

NIKERATOS: Blackmailer!

(Δη.)   καὶ σὺ γάρ.

(Νι.)   τὸ παιδίον
ἐξένεγκέ μοι.

(Δη.)   γελοῖον· τοὐμόν.

(Νι.)   ἀλλ' οὐκ ἔστι σόν.

(Δη.) ἐμόν.

(Νι.)   ἰώ' νθρωποι.

(Δη.)   κέκραχθι.

(Νι.)   τὴν γυναῖκ' ἀποκτενῶ   580
εἰσιών· τί γὰρ ποήσω;

(Δη.)   τοῦτο μοχθηρὸν πάλιν. (236)
οὐκ ἐάσω. ποῖ σύ; μένε δή.

(Νι.)   μὴ πρόσαγε τὴν χεῖρά μοι.

(Δη.) κάτεχε δὴ σεαυτόν.

(Νι.)   ἀδικεῖς Δημέα με, δῆλος εἶ,
καὶ τὸ πρᾶγμα πᾶν σύνοισθα.

(Δη.)   τοιγαροῦν ἐμοῦ πυθοῦ,
τῆι γυναικὶ μὴ' νοχλήσας μηδέν.

(Νι.)   ἆρ' ὁ σός με παῖς   585

584   οισθα B

DEMEAS: The same goes for you.

NIKERATOS: Bring out the baby to me.

DEMEAS: Don't be absurd. The baby's mine.

NIKERATOS: It isn't.

DEMEAS: It's mine.

NIKERATOS: Ho! People!

DEMEAS: Bawl your head off if you like.

NIKERATOS: I'll go inside and kill my wife. What else can I
   do?   580

DEMEAS: Trouble upon trouble! I won't let you. Stop!
  Wait! [*Makes to stop him.*]

NIKERATOS: Don't touch me!

DEMEAS: Control yourself.

NIKERATOS: You're cheating me. It's obvious. You're in
  the plot.

DEMEAS: Then find out about it from me. Don't trouble
  your wife.

NIKERATOS: Your son

ἐντεθρίωκεν;

(Δη.)   φλυαρεῖς· λήψεται μὲν τὴν κόρην,
                                                              (241)
ἔστι δ' οὐ τοιοῦτον. ἀλλὰ περιπάτησον ἐνθαδὶ
μικρὰ μετ' ἐμοῦ.

(Νι.)   περιπάτησον;

(Δη.)   καὶ σεαυτόν γ' ἀνάλαβε.
οὐκ ἀκήκοας λεγόντων, εἰπέ μοι, Νικήρατε,
τῶν τραγωιδῶν ὡς γενόμενος χρυσὸς ὁ Ζεὺς
                                        ἐρρύη 590
διὰ τέγους καθειργμένην τε παῖδ' ἐμοίχευσέν
                                        ποτε;   (246)

(Νι.) εἶτα δὴ τί τοῦτο;

(Δη.)   ἴσως δεῖ πάντα προσδοκᾶν· σκόπει,
τοῦ τέγους εἴ σοι μέρος τι ῥεῖ.

(Νι.)   τὸ πλεῖστον. ἀλλὰ τί
τοῦτο πρὸς ἐκεῖν' ἐστί;

(Δη.)   τότε μὲν γίνεθ' ὁ Ζεὺς χρυσίον,
τότε δ' ὕδωρ. ὁρᾶς; ἐκείνου τοὔργον ἐστίν.
   ὡς ταχὺ   595
εὕρομεν.

587-8 ενθαδιμικρα(μικρō C): μετεμου BC
588   περιπάτησον z: περιπατησω BC
590   οζευσχρυσος   B ?C

has cozened me! 585

DEMEAS: No! No! He'll take the girl — it's not like that.
Walk around for a bit with me.

NIKERATOS: 'Walk around'? [*They link arms and stroll round the stage together.*]

DEMEAS: Get a grip on yourself. Tell me, Nikeratos, haven't you heard the tragic actors saying how Zeus became gold and flowed through the roof and debauched a girl who had been 590
shut in?

NIKERATOS: What of it?

DEMEAS: Perhaps one ought to be ready for anything.
Consider whether some part of your roof leaks.

NIKERATOS: Most of it. But what has this to do with that?

DEMEAS: Sometimes Zeus becomes gold, sometimes rain.
You understand? It's his work. How quickly we discovered 595
it!

(Νι.)   καὶ βουκολεῖς με;

(Δη.)   μὰ τὸν ᾿Απόλλω, ᾿γὼ μὲν οὔ.
ἀλλὰ χείρων οὐδὲ μικρὸν ᾿Ακρισίου δήπουθεν εἶ·
                                                      (252)
εἰ δ᾿ ἐκείνην ἠξίωσε, τήν γε σήν –

(Νι.)   οἴμοι τάλας·
Μοσχίων ἐσκεύακέν με.

(Δη.)   λήψεται μέν, μὴ φοβοῦ
τοῦτο· θεῖον δ᾿ ἔστ᾿, ἀκριβῶς ἴσθι, τὸ
     γεγενημένον.   600
μυρίους εἰπεῖν ἔχω σοι περιπατοῦντας ἐν
     μέσωι   (256)
ὄντας ἐκ θεῶν· σὺ δ᾿ οἴει δεινὸν εἶναι τὸ
     γεγονός.
Χαιρεφῶν πρώτιστος οὗτος, ὃν τρέφουσ᾿
     ἀσύμβολον,
οὐ θεός σοι φαίνετ᾿ εἶναι;

(Νι.)   φαίνεται· τί γὰρ πάθω;
οὐ μαχοῦμαί σοι διὰ κενῆς.

(Δη.)   νοῦν ἔχεις, Νικήρατε. 605
᾿Ανδροκλῆς ἔτη τοσαῦτα ζῆι, τρέχει, πηδᾶι,
     πολὺ   (261)
πράττεται· μέλας περιπατεῖ· λευκὸς οὐκ ἂν
     ἀποθάνοι,
οὐδ᾿ ἂν εἰ σφάττοι τις αὐτόν. οὗτός ἐστιν –
     οὐ θεός;

NIKERATOS: You're having me on as well?

DEMEAS [*with false innocence*]: Far from it. You're just as
good as Akrisios, I think. If his daughter was honoured by
Zeus, perhaps your own daughter —

NIKERATOS: Ah! Moskhion has made a fool of me!

DEMEAS: He'll marry her. Don't worry. Rest assured, the
gods have brought about the present occurrence. I can tell
you of thousands going about in public who are children of   600
the gods! You think what has happened now strange. First
of all there's Khairephon. People feed him when he comes
to dinner without a contribution. Don't you think he's a
god?

NIKERATOS: He seems to be. What can I do? I'll not quibble
with you.

DEMEAS: Very sensible of you, Nikeratos. There's Androkles
too. Despite his age he runs and jumps and has a finger in   605
every pie. He walks around black. He wouldn't die white
even if someone were to slit his throat. He is — a god isn't
he?

ἀλλὰ ταῦτ' εὖχου γενέσθαι συμφέροντα, θυμία,
σφάττε· τὴ]ν κόρην μέτεισιν οὑμὸς ὑὸς αὐτίκα.

610

<Νι.> ἐξ ἀνάγκης ἐστί ταῦ[τ]α πομ[...].μ[.]ι

<Δη.>   ν[ο]ῦν ἔχει[ς.

(Νι.) εἰ δ' ἐλήφθη τότε –

(Δη.)   πέπαυσο· μὴ παροξύνου· πόει   (267)
τἄνδον εὐτρεπῆ.

(Νι.)   ποήσω.

(Δη.)   τὰ παρ' ἐμοῖ δ' ἐγώ.

(Νι.)   πόει.

(Δη.) κομψὸς εἶ – χάριν δὲ πολλὴν πᾶσι τοῖς θεοῖς
ἔχω
οὐθὲν εὑρηκὼς ἀληθὲς ὧν τότ' ὤμην γεγονέναι.

615

ΧΟΡΟΥ

606-11   om. B

88

But pray that this will turn out well. Burn incense,
  slaughter the victim. My son will soon come to fetch the
  girl.   610
NIKERATOS: ? I must . . . accept all this.
DEMEAS: You're very sensible.
NIKERATOS: But if he had been taken then —
DEMEAS: Stop! Don't get angry. Make your preparations
  inside.
NIKERATOS: I will.
DEMEAS: And I'll do the same in here.
NIKERATOS: Go ahead. [*He exits into his house.*]
DEMEAS: Well done! Thanks be to the gods that nothing of
  what I thought had happened has turned out to be true.   615
  [*He exits.*]

THE FOURTH CHORAL INTERLUDE

ΜΟΣΧΙΩΝ

ἐγὼ τότε μὲν ἧς εἶχον αἰτίας μάτην (271)
ἐλεύθερος γενόμενος ἠγάπησα καὶ
τοῦθ' ἱκανὸν εὐτύχημ' ἐμαυτῶι γεγονέναι
ὑπέλαβον· ὡς δὲ μᾶλλον ἔννους γίνομαι
καὶ λαμβάνω λογισμόν, ἐξέστηκα νῦν 620
τελέως ἐμαυτοῦ καὶ παρώξυμμαι σφόδρα (275)
ἐφ' οἷς μ' ὁ πατὴρ ὑπέλαβεν ἡμαρτηκέναι.
εἰ μὲν καλῶς οὖν εἶχε τὰ περὶ τὴν κόρην
καὶ μὴ τοσαῦτ' ἦν ἐμποδών, ὅρκος, πόθος,
χρόνος, συνήθει', οἷς ἐδουλούμην ἐγώ, 625
οὐκ ἂν παρόντα γ' αὖτις ἠιτιάσατο (281)
αὐτόν με τοιοῦτ' οὐδέν, ἀλλ' ἀποφθαρεὶς
ἐκ τῆς πόλεως ἂν ἐκποδων εἰς Βάκτρα ποι
ἢ Καρίαν διέτριβον αἰχμάζων ἐκεῖ·
νῦν δ' οὐ ποήσω διὰ σέ, Πλαγγὼν φιλτάτη, 630
ἀνδρεῖον οὐθέν· οὐ γὰρ ἔξεστ' οὐδ' ἐᾶι (286)
ὁ τῆς ἐμῆς νῦν κύριος γνώμης Ἔρως.
οὐ μὴν ταπεινῶς οὐδ' ἀγεννῶς παντελῶς
παριδεῖν με δεῖ τοῦτ', ἀλλὰ τῶι λόγωι μόνον,
εἰ μηθὲν ἄλλ', αὐτὸν φοβῆσαι βούλομαι 635
φάσκων ἀπαίρειν. μᾶλλον εἰς τὰ λοιπὰ γὰρ (291)
φυλάξεθ' οὗτος μηθὲν εἷς μ' ἀγνωμονεῖν,
ὅταν φέροντα μὴ παρέργως τοῦτ' ἴδηι.
ἀλλ' οὑτοσὶ γὰρ εἰς δέοντά μοι πάνυ
καιρὸν πάρεστιν ὃν μάλιστ' ἐβουλόμην. 640

622   οπατηρμ' B
637   θ' ουτος B: τ' ουτος C

ACT FIVE

[*Re-enter Moskhion from one of the side-entrances*]

MOSKHION:

    I was glad then when I was released from the false charge
that was made against me and I thought myself quite lucky.
Now that I've collected myself and thought the matter over,   620
I'm quite beside myself and extremely angry that my father
could have entertained that kind of suspicion about me. If
there was no problem about the girl and there weren't so
many obstacles in the way, the oath I swore, my love, the
time that has gone by, our relationship, to all of which I am
a slave, he wouldn't ever again have made such a charge   625
against me, face to face. Instead, I'd have disappeared from
the city, to Baktria perhaps or Karia, and would be spending
my time soldiering there. No such acts of bravery for me
now because of *you*, dearest Plangon. I cannot do such a
thing, nor does love, the master of my will, allow it. Even   630
so, I cannot overlook this slight and take my humiliation
lying down, even if my reaction is just a pretence. If nothing
else, I want to scare Demeas by pretending that I'm going   635
abroad. In future he'll take care not to behave so unsympathetically towards me, when he sees how seriously I take
this affront.

    [*He observes Parmenon entering by one of the side-
    entrances.*]

But here's Parmenon, just the man I want and just when I
want him.   640

Πα. νὴ τὸν Δία τὸν μέγιστον, ἀνόητόν τε καὶ   (296)
     εὐκαταφρόνητον ἔργον εἴμ' εἰργασμένος·
     οὐθὲν ἀδικῶν ἔδεισα καὶ τὸν δεσπότην
     ἔφυγον. τί δ' ἦν τούτου πεποηκὼς ἄξιον;
     καθ' ἓν γὰρ οὑτωσὶ σαφῶς σκεψώμεθα.   645
     ὁ τρόφιμος ἐξήμαρτεν εἰς ἐλευθέραν   (301)
     κόρην· ἀδικεῖ δήπουθεν οὐδὲν Παρμένων.
     ἐκύησεν αὕτη· Παρμένων οὐκ αἴτιος.
     τὸ παιδάριον εἰσῆλθεν εἰς τὴν οἰκίαν
     τὴν ἡμετέραν· ἤνεγκ' ἐκεῖνος, οὐκ ἐγώ.   650
     τῶν ἔνδον ὡμολόγησε τοῦτό τις τεκεῖν·   (306)
     τί Παρμένων ἐνταῦθα πεποίηκεν κακόν;
     οὐθέν. τί οὖν οὕτως ἔφυγες, ἀβέλτερε
     καὶ δειλότατε; γελοῖον. ἠπείλησ' ἐμὲ
     στίξειν· μεμάθηκας· διαφέρ[ει δ' ἀ]λλ' οὐδὲ
       γρῦ   655
     ἀδίκως παθεῖν τοῦτ' ἢ δικαίως. ἔστι δὲ   (311)
     πάντα τρόπον οὐκ ἀστεῖον.

(Μο.)   οὗτος.

(Πα.)   χαῖρε σύ.

(Μο.) ἀφεὶς ἃ φλυαρεῖς ταῦτα θᾶττον εἴσιθι
     εἴσω.

(Πα.)   τί ποήσων;

650   εκεινοσηνηγκ'·· Β
651   ωμολογηκε C
653   εφευγεσουτος Β: εφυγεσουτως C

PARMENON: [*not observing Moskhion*]: My god, I've done
a foolish and contemptible thing! Although quite innocent
I took fright and ran away from my master. What had I
done to justify running away? Let's go through the arguments one by one like this. Moskhion was indiscreet with   645
a citizen's daughter. I don't think *Parmenon* is to blame
here. She became pregnant. That's not *Parmenon's* fault.
The baby came into our house. He brought him, not I. One
of the household said she was the mother. What has   650
Parmenon to answer for here? Nothing. Why did you run
away like that, you foolish coward? It's laughable. He said
he would brand me. You understand now. There's nothing   655
to choose between a punishment you deserve and one you
don't. Whichever way you look at it, it's highly unpleasant.
MOSKHION: You there!
PARMENON: Hallo.
MOSKHION: Stop this nonsense and get inside quickly.
PARMENON: What for?

(Μο.)   χλαμύδα καὶ σπάθην τινὰ
ἔνεγκέ μοι.

(Πα.)   σπάθην ἐγώ σοι;

(Μο.)   καὶ ταχύ.   660

(Πα.) ἐπὶ τί;

(Μο.)   βάδιζε καὶ σιωπῆ τοῦθ' ὅ σοι   (316)
εἴρηκα ποίει.

(Πα.)   τί δὲ τὸ πρᾶγμα;

(Μο.)   εἰ λήψομαι
ἱμάντα –

(Πα.)   μηδαμῶς· βαδίζω γάρ.

(Μο.)   τί οὖν
μέλλεις; – πρόσεισι νῦν ὁ πατήρ· δεήσεται
οὗτος καταμένειν δηλαδή. δεήσεται   665
ἄλλως μέχρι τινός· δεῖ γάρ. εἶθ', ὅταν δοκῆ,
                                        (321)

πεισθήσομ' αὐτῷ. πιθανὸν εἶναι δεῖ μόνον
ὃ μὰ τὸν Διόνυσον οὐ δύναμαι ποεῖν ἐγώ.
τοῦτ' ἐστίν. ἐψόψηκε προϊὼν τὴν θύραν.

Πα. ὑστερίζειν μοι δοκεῖς σὺ παντελῶς τῶν ἐνθάδε
                                        670
πραγμάτων, εἰδώς τ' ἀκριβῶς οὐθὲν οὔτ' ἀκηκοὼς
                                        (326)
διὰ κενῆς σαυτὸν ταράττεις εἰς ἀθυμίαν τ' ἄγεις.

MOSKHION: Fetch me a cloak and sword.

PARMENON: A *sword*, for you?

MOSKHION: And hurry up about it!   660

PARMENON: Why do you want a cloak and sword?

MOSKHION: Go on. Do what I've told you and keep quiet
while you're doing it.

PARMENON: What's the game?

MOSKHION: If I get a rope, I'll —

PARMENON: No! No! I'm off. [*He enters the house.*]

MOSKHION: Why don't you get a move on then?

> [*Left alone he soliloquizes.*]

> Father will come now. Obviously he'll beg me to stay.
He'll do this unsuccessfully for a while. He must. Then,   665
whenever I want, I'll let myself be persuaded. I just have to
be convincing which, damn it, is the last thing I can be. This
is it. I hear the door.

PARMENON [*re-entering*]: You seem to be completely be-
hindhand with what's going on inside. You don't know and
you haven't heard anything accurate and that's why you're   670
putting yourself into unnecessary confusion and bringing
yourself to despair.

Μο. οὐ φέρεις;

(Πα.)   πooῦσι γάρ σοι τοὺς γάμους·
     κεράννυται,
     θυμιᾶτ', ἐνῆρκτ', ἀνῆπται σπλάγχνα θ'
        ῾Ηφαίστου φλογί.

(Μο.) οὗτος, οὐ φέρεις;

(Πα.)   σὲ γάρ, σὲ περιμένουσ' οὗτοι
     πάλαι.   675
     μετιέναι τὴν παῖδα μέλλεις; εὐτυχεῖς· οὐδὲν
        κακόν   (331)
     ἐστί σοι. θάρρει· τί βούλει;

(Μο.)   νουθετήσεις μ',
     εἰπέ μοι,
     ἱερόσυλε;

(Πα.)   παῖ, τί ποιεῖς, Μοσχίων;

(Μο.)   οὐκ εἰσδραμὼν
     θᾶττον ἐξοίσεις ἅ φημι;

(Πα.)   διακέκομμαι τὸ στόμα.

673   οινοσκεραν νυται C

674   θυμιατ' ανηπτ' ανηρ[[κ̣]]αι Β: θυμιαματ' ενηρκτ'
      αναπτεται C: σπλαγχναθ' ηφαισουπυρι φλογι B; θυματ'
      ηφαισουφλογι C

96

MOSKHION: What about the cloak and sword?

PARMENON: They really are starting the wedding. The wine's a mixing, the incense a burning. The sacrifice has started. The entrails are ablaze in the flame of Hephaistos.

MOSKHION: You there! What about the cloak and sword?

PARMENON [*ignoring Moskhion's question*]: It's you, *you* they're waiting for. They've been waiting for ages. Why don't you fetch the girl now? You're in luck. There's no trouble. Cheer up. Why worry?

675

MOSKHION: [*striking Parmenon across the face*]: Advise me, will you, you rogue?

PARMENON: Ah! What are you doing, Moskhion?

MOSKHION: Go inside and fetch out what I tell you to fetch out and be quick about it!

PARMENON: My lip's split.

(Μο.) ἔτι λαλεῖς οὗτος;

                          βαδίζω. νὴ Δὶ' ἐξεύρηκά γε 680
[Πα.] τόδε κακόν.

(Μο.)   μέλλεις;

(Πα.)   ἄγουσι τοὺς γάμους ὄντως.

(Μο.)   πάλιν; (336)
    ἕτερον ἐξάγγελλέ μοι τι. -νῦν πρόσεισιν· ἂν
        δέ μου
    μὴ δέητ', ἄνδρες, καταμένειν, ἀλλ' ἀποργισθεὶς
        ἐαῖ
    ἀπιέναι -τουτὶ γὰρ ἄρτι παρέλιπον -τί δεῖ
        ποεῖν;
    ἀλλ' ἴσως οὐκ ἂν ποήσαι τοῦτ'. ἐὰν δέ; πάντα
        γὰρ   685
    γίνεται· γελοῖος ἔσομαι, νὴ Δὶ' ἀνακάμπτων
        πάλιν.   (341)

Πα. ἤν· χλαμὺς πάρεστιν αὕτη καὶ σπάθη· ταυτὶ λαβέ.

(Μο.) δεῦρο δός. τῶν ἔνδον οὐθείς σ' εἶδεν;

(Πα.)   οὐθείς.

(Μο.)   οὐδὲ εἷς
    παντελῶς;

(Πα.)   οὔ φημι.

(Μο.)   τί λέγεις; ἀλλά σ' ὁ Ζεὺς ἀπολέσαι.

MOSKHION: Are you still talking?

PARMENON: I'm off. I've really brought this upon myself.   680

MOSKHION: Why don't you go?

PARMENON [*tamely as he departs*] : The wedding really is
   taking place.

MOSKHION: Still at it? Bring out some more news to me!
   Now he'll come. But, gentlemen, supposing he doesn't ask
   me to stay — I left this out of the reckoning just now —
   suppose he becomes angry and lets me go. What do I do
   then? Maybe he won't do that, but if he does, anything   685
   might happen. I'll be a laughing stock when I make an
   about turn.
      [*Re-enter Parmenon carrying cloak and sword.*]

PARMENON: There you are. Here's a cloak and a sword.
   Take them.

MOSKHION: Give them here. [*Moskhion takes the cloak and
   sword and puts on the cloak as he speaks.*] Did anybody
   inside see you?

PARMENON: Nobody.

MOSKHION: No one at all?

PARMENON: No.

MOSKHION: What are you saying? Damn you!

(Πα.) πρόαγ' ὅποι μέλλεις· φλυαρεῖς.

(Δη.)   εἶτα ποῦ' στιν, εἰπέ μοι;   690
παῖ, τί τοῦτο;

(Πα.)   πρόαγε θᾶττον.

(Δη.)   ἡ στολὴ τί βούλεται;
τί τὸ πάθος; μέλλεις ἀπαίρειν, εἰπέ μ[οι,
    ῠ –υ–

(Πα.) ὡς ὁρᾶς, ἤδη βαδίζει κἀστὶν ἐν ὁδω[ῖ. νῦν
    δὲ χρὴ
κἀμὲ τοὺς ἔνδον προσειπεῖν· ἔρχο[μ' ἤδη.

[Δη.]   Μοσχίων,
ὅτι μὲν ὀργίζει, φιλῶ σε, κοὐχ[695
εἰ λελύπησαι γὰρ ἀδίκως αἰτίαν.[
ἀλλ' ἐκεῖν' ὅμως θεώρει· τίνι πικρ[;
εἰμὶ γὰρ πατήρ· ε[.......]αλαβών σε παιδίον
ἐξέθρεψ'· εἰ σ..[......]ς γέγονεν ἡδὺς τοῦ
    βίου,
τοῦτόν εἰμ' ὁ δοὺς [ἔγωγε], δι' ὃν ἀνασχέσθαι
    σ' ἔδει   700
καὶ τὰ λυπήσαντα [παρ' ἐ]μοῦ καὶ φέρειν τι
    τῶν ἐμῶν
ὡς ἂν υόν. οὐ δικαίως ἡτιασάμην τί σε·
ἠγνόησ', ἥμαρτον, ἐμάνην. ἀλλ' ἐκεῖνο.[
εἷς γε τοὺς ἄλλους ἁμαρτὼν σοῦ πρόνοιαν
    ἡλίκη[ν

704   γε z: τε Β

100

PARMENON: Go wherever you want. You're being ridiculous.

[*Demeas comes out of his house, speaking back in to one of his slaves.*]

DEMEAS: Then where is he, tell me? 690

[*He turns and sees the strangely-attired Moskhion.*]

Good Heavens! What's this?

PARMENON [*to Moskhion*]: Go on, then, get a move on.

DEMEAS [*to Moskhion*]: Why are you dressed like that? What's wrong? You mean to leave Athens? Tell me . . .

PARMENON [*sarcastically to Demeas*]: As you can see, he's on the march and on his way. It's time for me to have a talk with the family. I'm off. [*Exit Parmenon into Demeas' house.*]

DEMEAS: Moskhion, I'm glad you're angry and I don't (. . .) If it hurt you to be accused unfairly . . . 695

But I'd like you to consider one point: for whom (. . .) bitter . . . I'm your father . . . I took you when you were a baby, I brought you up. If . . . you have had any pleasant . . . in your life, I'm the one who gave it to you. Because of this, you ought to have put up with anything I did to hurt you and tolerated any of my mistakes as a son would. I 700 accused you unfairly: I was misled, I was wrong, I was mad. But that . . . although I was wrong, what care I took about you regarding the outside world!

ἔσχον, ἐν ἐμαυτῶ τ' ἐτήρουν τοῦθ' ὃ δή ποτ'
   ἠγνόουν·   705
οὐχὶ τοῖς ἐχθροῖς ἔθηκα φανερὸν ἐπιχαίρειν·
   σὺ δὲ
τὴν ἐμὴν ἁμαρτίαν νῦν ἐκφέρεις καὶ μάρτυρας
ἐπ' ἐμὲ τῆς ἐμῆς ἀνοίας λαμβάνεις· οὐκ ἀξιῶ,
Μοσχίων. μὴ μνημονεύσηις ἡμέραν μου τοῦ βίου
μίαν ἐν ἧι διεσφάλην τι, τῶν δὲ πρόσθεν
   ἐπιλάθηι.   710
πόλλ' ἔχων λέγειν ἐάσω· καὶ γὰρ οὐ καλῶς ἔχει
πατρὶ μόλις πιθέσθ', ἀκριβῶς ἴσθι, τὸ δ'
   ἑτοίμως καλόν.

Νι. μὴ' νόχλει μοι· πάντα γέγονε· λουτρά,
     προτέλει', οἱ γάμοι·
     ὥστ' ἐκεῖνος, ἄν ποτ' ἔλθηι, τὴν κόρην
     ἄπεισ' ἔχων.
     παῖ, τί τοῦτο;

Δη.   οὐκ οἶδ' ἔγωγε, μὰ Δία.

(Νι.)   πῶς οὐκ οἶσθα σύ; 715
     χλαμύς· ἀπαίρειν οὑτοσί που διανοεῖται.

(Δη.)   φησὶ γοῦν.

(Νι.) φησὶν οὗτος; τίς δ' ἐάσει, μοιχὸν ὄντ'
     εἰλημμένον,
     ὁμολογοῦντ'; ἤδη σε δήσω, μειράκιον, οὐκ
     εἰς μακράν.

(Μο.) δῆσον, ἱκετεύω.

I kept to myself my error at that time. I did not publish it   705
for the delectation of my enemies. But you now are making
public my mistakes and finding witnesses for my folly. This
is wrong, Moskhion. Don't remember the one day in my
life when I made a mistake and forget all the days before   710
then. I could say much more, but I shall stop now. You
know full well that it's wrong to yield to a father grudgingly.
To give way readily is right.

> [*Nikeratos comes out of his house, addressing his wife.*]

NIKERATOS: Stop bothering me. Everything's been done:
bath, preliminary sacrifice, the wedding. Moskhion, if he
ever does come, can go away with the girl. [*He turns round,
sees Moskhion and reacts with surprise.*] Good heavens!
What's this?

DEMEAS: I've no idea.

NIKERATOS: What do you mean? There's a cloak. He   715
intends going abroad.

DEMEAS: That's what he says.

NIKERATOS: Says? Who will allow him, a self-confessed
adulterer who has been caught in the act. I'll tie you up
young man, and soon.

MOSKHION [*ironically, making as if to resist*]: Bind me, I
ask you to.

Νι.   φλυαρεῖς πρός μ' ἔχων. οὐ καταβαλεῖς
τὴν σπάθην θᾶττον;

(Δη.)   κατάβαλε, Μοσχίων, πρὸς τῶν θεῶν,
μὴ παροξύνηις.

Μο.   ἀφείσθω· καταλελιπαρήκατε   720
δεόμενοί μου.

(Νι.)   σοῦ δεόμενοι; δεῦρο δή.

(Μο.)   δήσεις μ' ἴσως;

(Δη.) μηδαμῶς. ἔξω κόμιζε δεῦρο τὴν νύμφην.

Νι.   δοκεῖ;

Δη. πάνυ μὲν οὖν.

Μο.   εἰ τοῦτ' ἐποίεις εὐθύς, οὐκ ἂν πράγματα
εἶχες, ὦ πάτερ, φιλοσοφῶν ἄρτι.

Νι.   πρόαγε δὴ σύ μοι –   725
μαρτύρων ἐναντίον σοι τήνδ' ἐγὼ δίδωμ' ἔχειν
γνησίων παίδων ἐπ' ἀρότωι, προῖκα τἀμὰ πάνθ'
   ὅταν
ἀποθάνω γ', ὃ μὴ γένοιτ', ἀλλ' <εἰσ>αεὶ ζωίην.

(Μο.)   ἔχω,
λαμβάνω, στέργω.

(Δη.)   τὸ λοιπόν ἐστι λουτρὰ μετιέναι·
Χρυσί, πέμπε τὰς γυναῖκας, λουτροφόρον,

NIKERATOS: You're still keeping up this nonsense? Won't
you hurry up and put down your sword?
DEMEAS: Put it down, Moskhion, please. Don't provoke
him.   720
MOSKHION [*discarding his sword*]: There you are. Your
entreaties have succeeded. You've persuaded me.
NIKERATOS: Entreaties? [*threateningly*] Come here!
MOSKHION: You're going to tie me up?
DEMEAS: Stop this! [*To Nikeratos*] Bring out the bride.
NIKERATOS: You think that's best.
DEMEAS: Yes indeed.
       [*Nikeratos returns to his house.*]
MOSKHION: If you'd done this at once, father, you wouldn't
have had the trouble of all that moralizing just now.
       [*Nikeratos re-enters with Plangon on his arm*].
NIKERATOS: Go ahead, girl.   725
       [*Bride and groom stand beside each other as Nikeratos
       pronounces the marriage-formula.*]
       Before witnesses I give you this girl to keep for the pro-
duction of a crop of legitimate children and I offer as dowry
all my property, whenever I die — which god forbid (— may
I live forever).
MOSKHION [*taking Plangon by the hand*]: I have,
I take, I cherish,
DEMEAS [*summoning his household*]: All that remains
is to fetch the bath-water for Moskhion. Khrysis, escort
the womenfolk, the water-carrier

αὐλητρίδα. 730
δεῦρο δ' ἡμῖν ἐκδότω τις δᾷδα καὶ
    στεφάνους, ἵνα
συμπροπέμπωμεν.

(Μο.)   πάρεστιν ὅδε φέρων.

(Δη.)   πύκαζε σὺ
κρᾶτα καὶ κόσμει σεαυτόν.

(Μο.)   ἀλλ' ἐγώ.

(Δη.)   παῖδες καλοί,
μειράκια, γέροντες, ἄνδρες, πάντες εὐρώστως
    ἅμα
πέμψ[α]τ' εὐνοίας προφήτην Βακχίωι φίλον
    κρότον. 735
ἡ δὲ καλλίστων ἀγώνων πάρεδρος ἄφθιτος θεὰ
εὐμενὴς ἔποιτο Νίκη τοῖς ἐμοῖς ἀεὶ χοροῖς.

ΣΑΜΙΑ

ΜΕΝΑΝΔΡΟΥ

and the musician. 730

    [*Khrysis and various other persons emerge from
    Demeas' house.*]

Someone bring out a torch and garlands so that we may
join the procession.

MOSKHION: Here he is. [*An attendant comes out with
torch and garlands.*]

DEMEAS: Deck your head and adorn yourself.

MOSKHION: I will.

DEMEAS [*turning to the audience*]: Lovely boys,
  young men, old men, gentlemen, all of you. Cheer-
  fully send forth applause, harbinger of goodwill,
  dear to the Bakchic one. May the attender of the
  fairest contests, immortal goddess Victory, follow 735
  my choruses with kindly intent.

    [*exeunt omnes.*]

ΑΠΟΣΠΑΣΜΑΤΙΟΝ ΑΜΦΙΣΒΗΤΗΣΙΜΟΝ

PHRYNICHVS, Εκλ. 157 Fischer.
λίβανον λέγε τὸ δένδρον, τὸ δὲ θυμιώμενον λιβανωτόν
...
Μένανδρος ἐν τῆι Σαμίαι φησί.
    φέρε τὴν λιβανωτόν· σὺ δ' ἐπίθες τὸ πῦρ, Τρύφη.

Fragment (Phrynikhos, *Eklogai* 157 Fischer):
    Bring the incense. You put the fire on the altar, Tryphe.

NOTES

ACT ONE

The speech of Moskhion, although it contains a great deal of expository material and at least two passages of audience address (see on 5 and 31-34), has greater claims to be called a monologue than a prologue. See Bain, 187f and cf. J.C.B. Lowe, *CR* n.s. 31 (1981) 9; 'to call his monologue a "prologue" encourages the unjustified assumption that all Menander's plays had a prologue'.

When the papyrus opens (only a few lines can be missing) Moskhion is discussing his own personal misfortune which he will describe in detail later (38ff.). In what has been lost he must have mentioned Demeas and made it clear that he was his adoptive father (cf. 346f. and note **my father's** in 6 and **after that** in 7).

5   **for you:** (plural) the audience.

10ff.   Although comparatively little is missing, these lines have not been restored or explained to general satisfaction. I have followed, without all that much confidence, the restorations accepted by W. Luppe, *ZPE* 20 (1976) 295f. and the interpretation offered by him. Against this it can be urged that we have to assume an adversative use of *mentoi* which is so far unparalleled in Menander (the discussion of this passage by M.H. de Kat Eliassen, *Symbolae Osloenses* 50 (1975) 61ff. does not convince me).

10   **I was enrolled into my deme:** at the age of eighteen every Athenian male was examined by the demesmen of his father and if accepted became an Athenian citizen. See Aristotle, *Constitution of Athens* 42.1. The trouble with the interpretation and restoration accepted here is, as Sandbach points out, that it is hard to see how on such an occasion any opportunity would have been afforded of *not* being one of the crowd.

13   **acting as a khorēgos:** providing financial backing for a choral or dramatic performance presented at some Athenian festival. By Menander's time the dramatic *khorēgia* at the city Dionysia had been abolished and the dramatic competition was the responsibility of a single public official, the *agōnothetēs*. What may be meant here is the fulfilment of some local *khorēgia*. For the implications about the wealth and social standing of Demeas' household provided by this and the other details in Moskhion's narrative – the family is very wealthy – see L. Casson, 'The Athenian Upper Class and New Comedy', *Transactions of the American Philological Society* 106 (1976) 290.

15   **I led my phyle:** he means he was cavalry commander for his 'tribe'. It seems surprising that so young a man should hold so important an office. Sandbach may well be right in thinking that by Menander's time such offices entailed ceremonial rather than military duties.

18   **well-behaved:** see note on 273.

21   **Samian courtesan:** Samos was notorious for its prostitutes. Other Menandrean hetairai came from there, Khrysis in his *Eunoukhos* (Terence's Thais) and the sisters in *Dis exapatōn* (the Bacchides of Plautus' play). On the reputation of Samos in antiquity see K. Tsantsanoglou, *ZPE* 12 (1973) 192f.

22   **it could have happened to anyone:** lit. 'a human occurrence perhaps'. This is a commonplace in erotic contexts: cf. Ter. *Ad*. 471, excusing an act of passion, *humanumst*.

23   **he was ashamed:** there is a kind of reverse of the norm here. In comedy the usual situation is that the son becomes infatuated with a courtesan or commits some peccadillo (like Aeschinus in Terence's *Adelphoe* and Moskhion in this play) and then is prevented by his shame from confessing to his father.

26ff.   punctuation and construction are uncertain here. In the following lacuna we must have been introduced to Nikeratos and his family (note **the girl's mother** in 36) and given an account of the joint departure of the two fathers.

31-34   are quite obscure, particularly in the phrase **smashing the seal** in 34. In 33 *-esthe* is the second person plural ending of a verb -aorist middle subjunctive or present subjunctive middle of an -eo verb? — a further address of the audience.

38   **from our farm**: the wealthy Demeas has an estate in the country as well as a town house. This is a common situation in New Comedy. It often assists the dramatist's plotting: e.g. in Terence's *Eunuch* where 'Simon's' prolonged absence in the country facilitates the amatory adventures of his sons. We do not know why Moskhion came back 'in a hurry'.

39   **the Adonis-festival**: as so often in New Comedy a girl is raped at a festival (cf. for example Pamphile at the Tauropolia in *Epitrepontes*), one of the few occasions where Athenian girls might be seen in public. This instance is somewhat different, since the festival takes place in a private house. The generally relaxed conditions of an orgiastic rite and a lack of the usual protection of the maiden would have given the young man his opportunities. The curious festival honouring Adonis, in which trays of forced vegetable produce and fruits (the 'gardens' referred to here) were carried on to house-roofs, became popular with women in Athens during the last quarter of the fifth century. For discussions of the Adonia see the works referred to in Gomme-Sandbach and Jacques: an adventurous treatment of the origin and meaning of the rite is found in E. Detienne, *The Gardens of Adonis : Spices in Greek Mythology* (tr. J. Lloyd), Hassocks, Sussex, 1977.

43   The test is doubtful here. See Sandbach whose bolder suggestion *oim' entheastēs* 'I became I suppose erotically possessed' is well worth considering.

48   For the text here, based on a suggestion made independently by Lowe and L.A. Post, see Lowe, 95f.

50ff.   Like Aeschinus in similar circumstances in Ter. *Adelphoe* 333ff. Moskhion does the decent thing; it could be said that he did not have very much choice. The girl, Plangon, was in a position to denounce him.

51   **first**: *proteros* = before they (the girl's family) approached me.

53   Again the text is very uncertain: for discussion see Sandbach, ad loc. and S.R. Slings, *ZPE* 30 (1978) 228 who suggests (unconvincingly to my mind) that we leave the rest of the line as it stands and restore the opening with (elliptical) *all' oun*: 'I promised to marry (if not right away) in any case after my father returned'. This would suggest misleadingly that Moskhion had a choice in the matter of marriage. Nikeratos' consent is essential.

53   **my father returned**: this raises the expectation that such a return will very soon take place. See R.L. Hunter, *Museum Helveticum* 37 (1980) 222f. Presumably the play is set at the beginning of the sailing season (for which see L. Casson, *Ships and Seamanship in the Ancient World*, Princeton 1971, 270ff.).

55   Restoration is uncertain here. See Sandbach ad loc. for a defence of what is printed here and for other views the authors cited in the introduction, p.xiv, n.2. In the lacuna Moskhion must have gone on to explain that the child had been taken into Demeas' house and that the plan was to tell Demeas that it was Khrysis' child. After this he would announce his intention of going to the harbour to inquire whether there was any news of his father's ship. Something may have been said about the slave Parmenon.

67   **I feel shame**: Moskhion reveals the major flaw in his character, a tendency to feel embarrassment and shame which produces unfortunate results. He cannot do what the situation demands (and what he never explicitly acknowledges), confess the whole truth to his father (he may fear that his father will say no to the marriage: he would be doing his father an injustice if that was the case). Nor, at the moment, as he makes explicit, can he do the second best, carry out the plot which the three conspirators have devised.

69	**You're only half a man!** this is a remarkable thing for a slave to say to a free man — in New Comedy the slave who like Parmenon is a confidant of the young master (*trophimos*) is often very frank with him — Parmenon uses the abusive vocative *androgyne*. In Aristophanes' speech in Plato's *Symposion* (189e) we are told that the word which originally meant 'hermaphrodite' was now only used as a term of abuse.
72	**that door:** a common situation for the lover in comedy who for some reason or other does not have access to (or is in some way alienated from) the one he loves (cf. Thrasonides in Men. *Mis.*A 6).
75	**went in:** I follow Lowe, 96 in assuming a hyperbaton here and referring the participle to Moskhion rather than to Parmenon himself.
77-8	A recapitulation of the intrigue.
84-85	**in a tenement:** Khrysis' sympathy for the child is notable in view of the tribulations she will undergo as a result of it. The poor mother of Herodas' third mimiambus lives in a tenement (Hdas. 3.47).
90	**more wretched:** the self-pitying Moskhion harks back to what he said in line twelve.
95	**to practise:** the verb restored denotes athletic training. Compare for the motif of withdrawal to a deserted spot to practise a speech Ter.*Andr.*406.
98ff.	I accept the bold and brilliant overruling of the papyrus attribution advocated by Sandbach (first in *Ménandre*, 121). It is based on the observation that elsewhere Nikeratos tends towards a staccato (à la Mr Jingle) style of speaking and on the consideration that the reference to the poor in line 101 would be more apt in the mouth of a speaker who is himself poor.
98	**rich:** the literal meaning 'fat' may be what is intended.
100	**wormwood:** a staple product of the area (used especially for medicinal purposes).
105	It is common in comedy to make reference to idle and dreamy slaves who do not act immediately when given orders. For a collection of such passages see D. Bain, *Masters, Servants and Orders in Greek Tragedy*, Manchester, 1981, 46 n. 3.
114	A new plot-strand is revealed. While abroad the two old men have decided that their children should marry. From now on we have two groups (Moskhion and his allies)(Demeas and Nikeratos) apparently working to the same end. We do not gather from what survives of the play what has led the two fathers to their decision. Possibly something was said in the lacuna at the end of this act. The exact nature of the relationship between the two older men remains dark. Is it a longstanding friendship? Has some act (in time of war or when they were abroad together?) by the poor man endeared him to the rich man and made him think it a good idea to join the two families by marriage?

123   **I began the sacrifice**: instead of practising his speech as he had intended, Moskhion began to day-dream. What follows is a series of details from the imagined wedding feast.

124   **the sacral water**: see the note on 713.

       [observing Demeas:] it is likely (but not quite certain) that Demeas was already on stage when Moskhion entered, too absorbed in his own thoughts to take note of him or of his soliloquy. Self-absorption of this kind is quite conceivable in Menander, cf. Men. *Epitr.* 419-35 and Bain, 138ff. If Demeas is present **I was a complete fool** might belong to him.

128   **He must have heard**: ambiguous. Either

       1) he must have heard my soliloquy. Or

       2) he must have heard that he now has an illegitimate son.

129   **You ask?**: the tone is sharp here. Demeas is well aware that Moskhion must know what Khrysis has done.

133   **good riddance**: lit. 'to the crows!' Common in comedy but not exclusively Attic: see Arkhilokhos fr. 196 A 31 West (*Delectus ex iambis et elegis Graecis*, Oxford, 1980).

135   **Do you really expect?**: the masculine *allōi* which is apparently offered by the Oxyrhynchus papyrus at the beginning of this line will not do. Demeas has no reason at this stage to doubt that he is the parent so that, if he did agree to bring up the child, there can be no question of some other *man* being involved. The suggestion that what he means is 'for Khrysis' and that he has used a generalizing masculine, thereby unconsciously hitting at the truth about the baby, seems to me far-fetched (see R. Kassel, *ZPE* 12 (1973) 8f.). I am not convinced by the defence of *allōi* put forward by E.G. Turner, *Scritti in onore de Orsolina Montevecchi*, Bologna, 1980, 413ff.

137f. and 140ff.: cf. the introduction,p.xix.

150   For the text here see Lowe, 97.

153   **I understand**: Demeas guesses that Moskhion is in love with Plangon (that this is what he believed is subsequently confirmed in 335).

157ff.: attribution is uncertain here. Sandbach's second thought (in Gomme-Sandbach) of giving 'I'll go in . . . I'll fetch the girl' all to Moskhion may be correct. **sprinkle myself with water** will refer to the groom's ritual purification: see on 713, Moskhion will perform this perfunctorily.

163f.   **the accidental . . . divinity**: for this (characteristically Greek) way of thinking and speaking see Dover, *GPM* 142f. In the ill-preserved conversation that follows, Demeas must have convinced Nikeratos that today was the day to hold the wedding.

190   **sesame seeds**: for the wedding cake.

194   **Bring a cook as well**: the Athenians (unless they happened to be athletes in training) tended to eat meat only on festal occasions and any other time a beast was required for sacrifice. On such occasions a professional was hired to deal with the slaughter, butchery and cooking. This individual becomes one of the regular types of New Comedy, a genre in which weddings are particularly frequent. He is also the person hired for the 'slap-up' dinner, the gourmet meal at which the principal delicacy is fish.

198   Parmenon may be talking to Khrysis. It is possible as Sandbach says that this is not a re-entry, but an utterance from inside heard through an open door.

200f.   **He'll have a job**: little does Demeas know!

201f.: why is Demeas in such a hurry (cf. 154)? Perhaps he is being depicted as naturally impulsive. On the other hand the desire on the part of fathers to see their sons settled down as soon as possible is a topic of comedy. Later in the play, after Demeas makes his discovery about the baby's parentage, his haste is easily explained.

ACT THREE

205ff. **. . . a fair voyage:** despite the fragmentary nature of this passage, the general sense is clear. After a sudden change of fortune which he is about to report, Demeas is comparing what has happened to him with the situation of sailors who after fair sailing in good weather encounter a great storm (a common image, cf. Eur. *Herakleidai* 427ff., Hor. *Od.*1.14.1ff., Ov. *Am.*2.9.31-2 of a metaphorical storm coming when the ship is almost in harbour).

207 For *exaiphnes. . . elthōn* cf. Homer, *Iliad* 9.6 [Boreas and Zephyros] *elthont' exapinēs.*

213 **if I am still seeing straight:** this is explained later when he tells us how he saw Khrysis nursing the baby (265ff., 278ff.).

216 Text and reading are uncertain here. For a justification of what is printed see *CGFPR* p. 187.

consider is addressed to the audience.

219 **As soon as . . . :** lit. 'for(gar) when . . .'. The form of Demeas' speech owes something to that of 'messenger' scenes in tragedy. Bad news is broken in a general way before an extended narrative explaining and justifying the speaker's gloom. Such narratives often begin like this with a phrase like 'when we . . .'. cf. Eur. *Med.*1136.

222 **basket:** this is the container of various objects need for the sacrifice which forms part of the marriage ceremony.

227 **flour:** 'wheat-meal'.

234 **weaving-room:** the form of this word *histeōn* did not endear Menander to Atticist grammarians (see the introduction,p.xxiv n.2): they state that the correct form is *histōn*. See G.P. Shipp, *Modern Greek Evidence for the Ancient Greek Vocabulary*, Sydney, 1981, 282f. Ironically the 'true' form, hitherto unattested in any Greek author, has turned up in a most unlikely place, an inventory of expenses from Egypt of the seventh-eighth centuries A.D. (PSI V 481 - see R. Pintaudi, *Aegyptus* 61 [1981] 97).

237 This woman though now free appears to be living in Demeas' house. Greek households sometimes resembled the populous establishments found in Chekhov replete with aged retainers and dependents taken in out of charity.

241 **talk:** *lalein* which in classical Greek means 'chatter' is common in Menander and later Greek as simply *talk*) (*say*. See Shipp (cited in the note on 234) 335.

248 Nothing of what the nurse says in the lacuna that follows can have made clear to Demeas the identity of the mother of the child: perhaps she says something that gives misleading confirmation of Khrysis' motherhood.

252 **dearie me!:** *o talan/talan* are expressions used only by women (or by men imitating women) in Greek comedy. The vocative form is used as an exclamation. See C. Dedoussi, *Hellenika* 17 (1964) 1ff. (Also *Dodone* 6 (1978) 22) and V. Schmidt, *Sprachliche Untersuchungen zu Herondas*, Berlin, 1968, 37.

255 **wretched woman:** *dysmore* this on the face of it high-flown word is in Menander like *ō talan* exclusively the property of women though it is much less common (something has gone wrong with the references in Sandbach's note here: they should be *Sam.* 69,370 *bis*, *Epitr.* 468).

256 **the master's:** lit. 'he himself' a manner used by slaves of referring to their master (cf. Latin *ipse*). Later Khrysis is referred to as *autē* (258).

257 **stopped whispering:** the girl now 'puts on an act' speaking louder so that the eavesdropper she knows to be present may hear her. See, for an anticipation of this technique in tragedy, Soph. *El.*1323ff. (cf. Bain, 81). She drops her voice again in what follows.

263   **quite calmly**: a kind of postponed stage-direction which enables the reader to visualize how Demeas made his entrance at the (lost) opening of the act.

269   **or - :** Demeas, unable in this context to come right out and utter his son's name, breaks off and, as actors often do at emotional moments in comedy (see Bain, 206), establishes a close contact with the audience (cf. 216, 329, 447, 683). Here **gentlemen**, the standard term for addressing the audience, is used.

273   **well-behaved**: Demeas uses the word that Moskhion used of himself.

278   **forced me**: is this an exaggeration on the part of Demeas or does it reflect something we are to imagine as having occurred off stage? Since Demeas decides to accept the child after Moskhion's speech in act two and as Khrysis does not really have any standing in the matter, one must, I think, convict Demeas of a distortion of the truth. He is victimising Khrysis.

285   **chopping up**: (cf. also 293) it is a traditional joke of comedy that the verb denoting butchery (for the mageiros as butcher see on 194) should be used applied to the cook in the metaphorical sense 'tire out', 'bore to death'. This cook displays one of the regular features of cooks in comedy, inquisitiveness (cf. Karion at the beginning of *Epitrepontes*, Men. *Epitr.* frr. 1,2) although up to now his questioning might be excused in that he is merely seeking information essential to the proper discharge of the task for which he has been hired. Later, in 369ff., he will also behave in an officious and interfering manner, be *periergos*.

    you don't know the trade: the cook is proud of his own professional status.

290   **table-layer**: another stock character of New Comedy. He assists the cook and serves the meal. The Bodmer codex has provided a splendid example of such a personage in the amoral and heartless Thracian of Men. *Asp.* 233ff.

296   **yes**: on *naikhi*, a word of curious distribution (in Old Comedy only in the mouth of a barbarian, frequent on vase graffiti and found in erotic epigram, once in Sophokles and a couple of times in Menander), see K.J. Dover, in *Classical Contributions* (Studies in honour of M.F. McGregor) Locust Valley, N.Y. (1981) 20.

301   **banging the door**: there are a number of passages in Greco-Roman comedy where reference is made to the noise of the house-door. Those where, as here, the perfect of the verb *plēssō* (which is not a synonym of *koptō*, the regular verb for knocking on a door) is found are best explained by the assumption that the reference is to the person coming out of the house noisily knocking upwards the bolt on the inside of the door. (It used to be believed, contrary to archaeological evidence, that the house-door opened outwards and that people knocked on their doors before opening them to warn passers by in the street). Often a sense of urgency attends these entrances. Parmenon perhaps comes out with a hint of a swagger. His confidence will soon turn out to be misplaced. See B. Bader, 'The ψόφος of the House-Door in Greek New Comedy', *Antichthon* 5 (1971) 35ff.

302f.   **the old woman**: presumably the nurse we met in Demeas' monologue. The pottery her interest will focus on will contain wine. It is a traditional assumption of comedy that women, particularly old women, are very fond of drink.

305f.   Demeas' statement naturally comes as a bolt from the blue for the unsuspecting Parmenon.

309f.   Strings of oaths are associated with Old Comedy (cf. Ar. *Birds* 194). Perhaps this is the kind of thing one might expect from a slave. There are no examples in New Comedy of a free man resorting to a string of asseverations.

312   **never**: Attic prose of the fourth century uses *mēdepote* rather than *mēpote* and one suspects that the solemnity of the (intended) oath has helped determine the form. See Dover (cited on 297) p. 19 (cf. Men. *Asp.* 283).

313ff.   Demeas proceeds in quite the wrong way in his interrogation of Parmenon and ends by having his own misconceptions confirmed as the truth:
Q. Who is the baby's mother? A. Khrysis (Parmenon sticking to the story).

Q. Who is the father? A. You, she says.

When Demeas then goes on to say that he knows the truth, Parmenon would then undoubtedly, if questioned correctly, have revealed the true state of affairs. Demeas, however, by saying only that he knows that Moskhion is the father and by not enquiring further about the mother leaves himself open to misunderstanding. Parmenon assumes that if Demeas knows that Moskhion is the father he must also know that Plangon is the mother. All that he is actually asked to agree to is Moskhion's share in the matter and this simply confirms to Demeas that he has been cuckolded.

320   Parmenon is prevent from saying what Moskhion later manages to say (529).

321   **a rope:** for beating him rather than **tying** him up. cf. 662f.

323   **brand:** it was common to brand a runaway slave's forehead: hence the abusive term *stigmatiās*.

325f.:   It is common in tragedy for characters in distress to call the elements or their physical surroundings to witness (cf. Eur. *Hipp.* 601 with Barrett's note). Demeas feels moved to follow their practice. A note in the right hand margin of B tells us that **O Citadel of Kekrops' land** etc. comes from Euripides' (lost) *Oidipous* (presumably an apostrophe since that play was set in Thebes): Euripides was very fond of apostrophising the *aithēr* (upper air). Demeas, unlike Nikeratos in the next act, is able to set things in proportion, come down from his tragic heights and apply himself to the matter in hand. He checks himself with a harangue in the second person. This is a common device in monologues in New Comedy (see Blundell, 65ff.). It is more appropriate in the mouth of a passionate young man than of a gray-beard. This is another example of the reversal of roles that is a motif of this play (see on 23).

337   **Helen:** par excellence the unfaithful wife of antiquity.

341   **strong wine:** (lit. *undiluted wine* — the ancients added water to their wine, cf. 392). Some excuse for sexual misdemeanours is afforded to young men in New Comedy if they have been drinking (but not always, cf. Philippides fr. 26). N.B. the mitigation of Aeschinus' rape of Philumena in *Adelphoe*: 'persuasit nox amor uinum adulescentia:/*humanumst*' (Ter. *Ad.*470f.). In reality Moskhion is not entitled to be given the benefit of this excuse.

344   **well-behaved:** cf. 273.

348   **a common whore:** an abusive word hurled quite unfairly at Khrysis: its literal meaning is 'beaten upon the ground'.

349   **now you must be a man:** this is the kind of thing normally said by a *young* lover in comedy.

360   **what's up!** on the exclamation *ti touti pai*, in which it is doubtful whether *pai* has anything to do with *pais* and certain in some instances that it cannot have the force of a vocative (because there is no one answering to that description present when it is uttered), see Sandbach ad loc.

361   **some old madman:** the cook did not observe Demeas when he first arrived earlier in this act. Hence he does not know that the man who has just rushed in is the man who hired him.

366f.   see on 301.

368   **I'll stand aside a little:** a 'stage-directional' phrase, on which see Bain, 152f. Perhaps it is suitable to a self-important person (cf. Sandbach, on 368) who wishes to keep the audience informed of his every move.

369ff.   A famous scene, illustrated on the Mytilene mosaic (see the introduction p.xxiv). Misunderstanding persists, *agnoia* rules. Demeas by refusing to make quite explicit his reasons for ejecting Khrysis — he assumes that as the guilty party she must be well aware of them — further postpones the revelation of the truth. It may be that his refusal is determined by reasons of security — ensuring no one overhears him mentioning Moskhion's dalliance with Khrysis — since the cook has retreated and Demeas may be unaware of his presence (374 comes *before* the cook draws attention to himself). Perhaps he is so deeply hurt by the wrong he thinks that Khrysis has done him that he cannot bring himself to spell out the painful facts.

369f. Khrysis uses two characteristically feminine expressions, *ō talan* and *dysmore* (see the notes on 252 and 255).

373 **the old woman:** the nurse or some attendant Khrysis brought with her when she first came to Demeas' house? Tryphe?

374-5 For the attribution here and the insertion of *ou* (implied by C and advocated by R. Ellis and Körte) see R. Merkelbach, *ZPE* 19 (1975) 203 who notes that added point is given to Demeas' *manthaneis* in 378 if Khrysis says *ou manthanō* here.

379 **I was everything to you:** cf. Diogenes Laertius, 6.96 'to her [Hipparkhia] Krates was everything'.

382 **servants:** I take this to be a rhetorical plural (the reference is to the old woman of 373) : Demeas is less than frank when dealing with the woman he loves. For the plural see J.-M. Jacques, p. 25 n. 2 and D. Del Corno, *Studi classici ed orientali* 24 (1975) 42.

382 Plausible cases can be made out for either of the alternative ways of interpreting the letters *khrysi* in this line:

1) they might well be the vocative of Khrysis – the hiatus following them is easy to justify (see V. Schmidt, cited on 252, 94) and Demeas tends in this scene to throw in Khrysis' name by way of reproach (378, 382, 392).

2) alternatively, they represent the elided neuter plural of *khrȳsion*, 'golden finery' or (less probably) 'gold coins'.
Jewellery and servants are often juxtaposed when women's property is mentioned. Demeas would be reminding Khrysis of his generosity in saying that he was letting her depart along with the jewellery *he* had given her.

385 **and will thank the gods for it:** lit. 'will offer sacrifice', a way of expressing the notion of being grateful. cf. 'sacrifice to me' = 'you can thank me' at Herodas 6.10.

391ff. Demeas affords Khrysis a bleak prospect of the career she will now pursue as a prostitute plying for hire, drinking herself to death at symposia.

398 **stay there:** as Demeas starts back into his house, Khrysis makes a move to follow or at least detain him. He checks her harshly.

399ff. The re-entrance of Nikeratos (he left sometime towards the end of the second act) carrying a scrawny sheep provides a completely new turn and helps lighten the atmosphere. Jokes about the poor sort of sacrificial victim that will be offered are traditional in comedy. Note the niggardly speaker of Antiphanes (a poet of 'middle' comedy) fr. 206.

400f. **the gods and the goddesses:** the addition of '**and the goddesses**' makes this a liturgical phrase.

401 Thanks to Prometheus (see Hesiod, *Theogony* 507ff. and West's note ad loc.) the unappetising and inedible portions of the victim go to the gods. This was taken by comic poets to be an indication of men's meanness in sacrificing. On the gods' part see K. Meuli, *Gesammelte Schriften* II, Zürich 1975, 935ff.

402 **a big spleen:** the victim as well as lacking flesh is diseased.

403 The practice of sending to absent friends left overs from the wedding feast is well attested. The idea suggested by Nikeratos reflects the 'Galgenhumor' of a poor man.

405f. **Is this Khrysis . . . standing in front of the door?** by assembling parallels from Roman Comedy and Lucian, Lowe, 97f. shows that this should be interpeted as a question. For this formulaic type of indication that a speaker is aware that someone else is present cf. Ter.*Eun.*848 'sed estne haec Thais, quam uideo? ipsast.'

411 **lunacy:** I follow Sandbach in Gomme-Sandbach in assuming that this refers to Khrysis' acceptance of the child. Nikeratos' view would not have seemed eccentric or particularly harsh to the Athenian audience.

413 For the attribution adopted here see R. Merkelbach, *ZPE* (1975) 208.

417 **the Pontos:** Nikeratos harks back to a theme which he had already exploited (in his laconic manner) in 98ff.

on the metrical form of this act see the introduction, p.xx).

421   **you'll finish me off**: Nikeratos uses this verb again at 544. The metaphor derives from torture. We infer that Nikeratos' wife has been pestering him and insisting that he go to Demeas and demand that Khrysis be reinstated. His next words show that her persistence has succeeded.

427   **Demeas is behaving without any sensitivity**: the literal meaning of *skatophagei* is 'he is eating dung'. When not merely being used as terms of abuse, this word and its derivatives describe starkly insensitive behaviour. Ironically, Demeas is later to describe Nikeratos in similar terms (550).

    my word: lit. 'by Poseidon and the gods'. This common type of reinforced oath 'by x and (other) gods' is used only by men.

428   **for his stupidity**: for *skaios* = left-handed >clumsy> stupid, see G.W. Bond on Euripides, *Herakles* 683 (he misinterprets this passage).

    We last saw Moskhion in the second act (161f.) when he departed (presumably in the direction of the agora) so as not to be in the way of the wedding preparations.

429   **I'll go and take my third bath**: Moskhion has been killing time in a bath house (*balaneion*) on which see R. Ginouvès, *Balaneutiké*, Paris, 1962, 183ff. or perhaps, as would suit a young man of his social status, a gymnasion (Ginouvès, op. cit. 129ff.). This has nothing to do with the ritual bath that forms part of the marriage ceremony (see the note on 713).

431   The absence of any acknowledgement of Nikeratos' greeting and the direct question he immediately puts indicate Moskhion's preoccupation with Plangon and his marriage to her.

434   **unpleasant**: *aēdia* can mean 'unpleasant behaviour': cf. P. Tebtun. 793 xi.5 (a petition complaining about violence) 'and unpleasantness having arisen, Dorion cut his lip . . Hesiod cut Dorion's right ear clean off'.

439   A piece of simultaneous action takes place on stage. Nikeratos who was presumably going to say something like 'then you had better approach Demeas' and Moskhion continue their conversation after Demeas' sudden arrival, but we do not hear them again until 451 when Nikeratos becomes audible once more. See Bain, 168f.

440   Demeas' opening words reveal the despondency that has overcome his household following the ejection of Khrysis. The serving women are inactive and weep: the wedding preparations make no progress.

444   **Dear Apollo**: he is addressing Apollo 'of the street', a statue of the deity which as a rule stood outside the front door of Athenian houses and is often the object of address in Greek drama. See Sandbach on *Dysk.* 659.

447   **gentlemen**: Demeas re-establishes the contact he made with the audience during the monologue which began the previous act. See Bain, 206 and Blundell, 41.

454   **someone is sending ambassadors to me**: that 'someone' is Khrysis. *presbeuein* means 'to go as an ambassador'. The middle voice used here has as its subject the sender of the embassy, either a state or (as here) an individual. See Sandbach, ad loc. and J. Wackernagel, *Vorlesungen über Syntax* 1, Basel, 1926, 126 (LSJ are in error).

456   **he too is wronging me**: earlier Demeas had convinced himself that Moskhion was Khrysis' innocent victim (327ff. **Moskhion has done you no wrong . . .**). Hence it comes as a tremendous shock to him to find Moskhion coming forward to speak on her behalf.

    what are you saying?: this is a very plausible supplement. It is not quite clear whether we should assume that Moskhion has not properly heard Demeas' aside or whether his reaction is a surprised response to the unsatisfactory reply given by Demeas in 455. Unaware of what Demeas has already discovered, Moskhion finds his behaviour completely irrational. See Bain, 125f. and the note below on 544.

457   **he ought to have rejoiced**: Moskhion's ready acceptance of the proposed marriage had convinced Demeas that he was anxious to escape the clutches of Khrysis (336f. **wishing to escape my Helen**).

459   **(I expect they'll) —** : in B the last two letters before the proper name are (probably) a kappa and an ōmega. Hence the restoration *prosdokō* . Demeas means to answer Moskhion by saying 'I expect our friends will thoroughly approve of what I'm doing' but checks himself. Although he believes himself to be entirely in the right, he does not wish to become involved in a debate, but rather to carry out his resolve of 446f. Moskhion must, he assumes, eventually desist because he must be aware that he is in the wrong.

461   **This is the limit**: lit. 'this is excess!'. Two restorations are possible in this line. If we adopt the singular *horais*, Demeas is addressing himself. With the plural verb (*horāth'*) he is bringing in the audience as witnesses. In the latter case he would be resuming a contact with them that began (in this act) at 446. Perhaps it is best to regard all of Demeas' asides in this scene as involving the audience. See Blundell, 41.

462   **worse than the other things!**: lit. 'more terrible than those terrible things'; Demeas means that, while it is bad enough to be cuckolded by one's son, it is even worse when your son tries to prevent you from breaking with the guilty woman.

464   **Go in**: Nikeratos ignores this instruction. His subsequent presence is to prove a great embarrassment to Demeas and Moskhion in the brilliant scene that follows. The reader should always remember how much each of the participants knows about what the others know of the true state of affairs and be aware of precisely which delusion each party harbours.
Demeas is half right: he believes that Moskhion has fathered a baby. He mistakenly thinks, however, that Khrysis is the mother. Hence everthing that Moskhion says in defence of Khrysis seems to him perfectly scandalous.
Moskhion, unaware of the incident inside Demeas' house which led him to his suspicions about the paternity of the child, believes that Demeas has suddenly changed his mind about accepting 'Khrysis' bastard' and seeks but does not find a rational explanation for his change of course.
Nikeratos shares the same misapprehension, but, of course, unlike Moskhion is completely in the dark about the parentage of the child.

465   **Moskhion, let me, let me, Moskhion**: the chiastic word order (ABBA) of the Greek is reproduced *Moskhion, eā m', eā me, Moskhion*), an emotive device of popular eloquence. See Eduard Fraenkel, *Kleine Beiträge zur klassischen Philologie* II, Roma, 1964, 119 who adduces the locus classicus for this phenomenon, Polemon's impassioned cry at Men. *Pk.*506f. *Glykerā kataleloipe me, kataleloipe me Glykerā.*

466   **I know everything**: Demeas believes that this should surely prove sufficient to make Moskhion change his tune. Any further persistence would be incredible.

473   **Isn't it clear?**: Demeas can stand Moskhion's effrontery no longer. He turns away from him and makes a further appeal to Apollo (see the note on 444).

476   **this way**: Demeas, thinking perhaps that even now Moskhion does not realise that he does indeed know everything (as Demeas thinks) about the child and its parentage, makes a last, desperate attempt to show him that the situation is hopeless and that for Khrysis the game is up. It is of course vital that Nikeratos should not know that Moskhion has fathered an illegitimate baby — the marriage to Plangon will be off if he gets to know of this — and in order to prevent him learning of this Demeas withdraws and beckons to Moskhion to follow him so that they may converse out of earshot. See Bain, 169ff.

477-79   Demeas in trying to explain himself to Moskhion unwittingly chooses a form of words which does not make it clear what he really knows about the baby. Moskhion taking him at his word and accepting that he knows *everything* — Parmenon he believes will have confessed all — still cannot understand Demeas' present attitude towards *Khrysis*. Anger at his own behaviour he could understand.

478   **one who knows**: Demeas had used the same expression of Parmenon in 317.

481   There is an attractive alternative to the text printed here. One might with Blume, 187 n. 35 follow those who adhere to what is implied by B, delete the second *ouden* and take the dikōlon after the first *ouden* as an indication of change of speaker. *Nothing* would then be Moskhion's answer to his own question. *In that case is Khrysis doing you wrong?* The following verb (on either interpretation the plural indicates *you and Khrysis*) would then be an imperative, *have a care*!

      You scum!: *katharma su* is an extremely abusive expression for a father to use when addressing his son. *katharma* means anything that is removed by cleaning, 'dirt', 'rubbish', and often has a ritual connotation. It develops into a strong term of abuse. Note Demosthenes' use of it when addressing Aiskhines (see Dem. 18.128 and Wankel ad loc.). The form of the expression, vocative + su, is hardly polite.

484   The absence of median diaeresis here (see the introduction, p.xx) is a deliberate effect, meant to suggest Demeas' agitation.

486   **thousands**: lit. 'ten thousand'. The Greeks were always ready to make the point that any given form of human activity or experience had been performed or had happened to others in time past and that, therefore, our view of any act presently being performed ought to be conditioned by a sense of proportion. This type of argument was used particularly when the bereaved were being consoled, but it was also applicable in a situation like this to mitigate the harshness of someone's reaction to an act of uncontrolled sexual passion. To cuckold one's father, however, was an act that no such argument or indeed no argument at all might justify.

488   **witnesses**: lit. 'those present'. The reference can only be to the audience (cf. 461) since Nikeratos is not involved in this conversation.

489   **Tell Nikeratos**: Moskhion is naturally taken aback by what he thinks is being suggested. It is certainly *deinon* to go up to your prospective father-in-law and inform him that some time last year you raped his daughter.

490   **it's so dreadful**: Demeas half-echoes what Moskhion said in 486.

491   **once he finds out**: Moskhion's prediction is immediately fulfilled.

492   Nikeratos, at last aware of what is being discussed — the 'aside' conversation has been a noisy one (cf. 481) — bursts into the argument and, predictably, becomes more excitable and less controllable than the other two participants.

495   Nikeratos thinks of three of the great sexual malefactors of heroic legend and tragedy:
        a) Tereus, seducer of his sister-in-law (he also cut out her tongue to prevent her revealing his misdeed).
        b) Oidipous, incestuous husband of his mother.
        c) Thyestes, seducer of his brother's wife.

498   **you durst**: the verb does not belong to the spoken language or to prose. Nikeratos is beginning to rant.

      Amyntor: the step-father who unjustly suspected his step-son Phoinix of seducing his concubine and in some versions of the story (e.g. Euripides' lost *Phoinix*) had him blinded.

502   What Demeas has been trying to prevent has now happened.

503   **into one's lap, as they say**: understand 'one must spit', a gesture to appease Adrasteia (=Nemesis), the goddess of resentment.

504   **Diomnestos**: it has not been established to whom this refers and why this person was regarded as an unsuitable son-in-law.

507 **couch:** Nikeratos uses the poeticism *lektron* (cf. 498 and 517).

510 **barber's shop:** mention of this jars with the tragic diction found elsewhere in Nikeratos' mouth. In antiquity barbers' shops were notorious sources of gossip. Polybios (3.20.5) refers to the efforts of two lesser historians as 'barber's shop tattle'.

513 **murder:** a further example of Nikeratos' hyperbolic mode of speaking and thinking. This was the kind of gross exaggeration that was frequently heard in Athenian law courts — see Dover, *GPM* 55.

515 **dried up:** with fright.

517 **halls:** the word *melathrois*, absurd as a description of Nikeratos' humble abode, belongs to lyric and tragedy and so does its scansion. Normally a syllable containing a short vowel which precedes mute and liquid is pronounced short. When as here we meet the artificial long pronunciation, we know that tragedy is being evoked. See Sandbach, *Ménandre*, 124.

519 **no Greek, a true Thracian:** addressed to Moskhion. Thracians were notorious for their sexual appetite.

520 **listen father:** Moskhion has begun to realise that his father does not know the truth and to guess what he suspects. With Nikeratos out of the way, he makes his confession.

521 This line is corrupt (see the apparatus). The restoration adopted here is likely to be correct, but cannot be considered absolutely certain.

523 **rearing:** the verb *trephō* applied to Khrysis here is not sufficient to prove that Khrysis had herself recently lost a baby and was capable of breast-feeding Moskhion's baby. The word does not inevitably have this connotation even when used with a woman as subject. So at Aiskhylos, *Khoephoroi* 750 the old nurse's *exethrepsa* does not show she was a wet-nurse or discredit the claim Klytaimestra makes in 897.

526f. The graver accusation is that of cuckolding his father, the lesser is the true one that he had raped Plangon.

530 **cheat:** the verb *boukolein* which is also used by Nikeratos (at 595) means literally 'tend cattle'. It is not obvious how it acquired its metaphorical meaning.

532 **but the door — :** lit. 'but someone the door . . .'. Before Demeas can supply the verb to complete his utterance, Nikeratos is on stage. It is clear from 555 that Demeas intended to say 'has struck'. See the note on 301.

Ah me! Ah me!: Nikeratos has had a nasty shock, experiencing something similar to what happened to Demeas before the beginning of act three. His language in this scene again aspires to the heights although not much of what he says is explicitly tragic (note, however, the absence of the article with the body-part *kardiān* in 534). In his distress he does not notice that he is not alone.

536 **so it's true:** this is best assigned to Demeas (assuming a missing dikōlon in 536).

542 **perhaps:** *tykhon*, the aorist participle neuter of *tynkhanein*, is used from the early fourth century onwards (first perhaps in the *Dissoi Logoi* 7.4) as a synonym for *isōs*. Menander often uses it in combination with *isōs* (as in 543). See H. Wankel on Demosthenes, 18.221.

544 **What are you saying?:** Nikeratos has not heard enough of Demeas' last utterance to make sense of it. See Blundell, 55 n. 28.

546 **drivel:** lit. 'you have a running nose', a common metaphor for nonsensical or foolish talk.

546 **story:** i.e. 'it's a fact', the familiar *logos vs ergon* contrast.

547 **you know:** *to deina* in this case is the something I do not want to specify by name. See Lowe, 101.

my dear fellow: the characteristically Attic form of address, *ō tan*, of unexplained etymology (it is not a contraction of *ō talan*: see G. Björck, *Das Alpha Impurum*, Upsala, 1950, 277), is rarely used without a touch of condescension.

549	**gets to know:** the truth which will inevitably out, that his daughter is the mother of Moskhion's baby. (Demeas echoes his son's words of 491f.).
550	**independent:** for a full discussion of the untranslatable word *authekastos* see Sandbach ad loc.
551	I follow Lowe, 98f. in treating this line as a rhetorical question rather than a statement.
	harbour such suspicions: those he had against Khrysis and Moskhion, cf. 538.
555	**banged the door:** see on 301.
556	Demeas (549f.) thought that he and Moskhion would become the targets of Nikeratos' rage. Instead, after Khrysis, unaware of what Demeas now knows and, persisting in her story, persuades Nikeratos' family to help her, it is the womenfolk who suffer.
567	**Apollo!:** see on 444.
568	Khrysis' language suggests tragedy.
569	**my baby:** Khrysis somewhat unnecessarily maintains the pretence (or is this a slip on Menander's part?).
	run inside: Khrysis does not obey Demeas' order. She is still there to be addressed at 574, 575. Because she does not realise that Demeas now knows she is innocent, she hesitates to return to the house from which she was so recently ejected.
573	The tradition displays an interesting variation here. B *and* C (see H. Riad, *ZPE* 11 (1973) 208) offer 'I am mad' which, if said by Demeas, must be the equivalent of 'my blood boils'. In B the variant 'never/don't' is written above 'I am mad'.
575ff.	Sticks are raised, physical contact is established and the two elderly men face up to each other and bandy accusations.
	1) Nikeratos accuses Demeas of assault.
	2) Demeas answers by saying that Nikeratos has been using violence against a free woman.
	3) Nikeratos says Demeas is a *sȳkophantēs* (a blackmailing accuser – see N.R.E. Fisher, *Social Values in Classical Athens*, London, 1976, 36).
	4) Demeas replies in kind.
	5) Nikeratos demands the baby.
	6) Demeas says it belongs to him.
580	Demeas' last assertion causes Nikeratos to appeal to witnesses (cf. 487). Since there are none present – and Nikeratos does not apparently have the kind of rapport with the audience acquired by Demeas (if this were audience address the vocative expression would be *andres*) – he attempts to summon them by crying *iō'nthrōpoi*. *iō* is very common in appeals for aid. We have examples in petitions from Ptolemaic Egypt of the use of the phrase *boān anthrōpous* when help is summoned or people called to witness an injury. See D. Bain, *ZPE* 44 (1981) 169ff., ibid. 45 (1982) 270.
584	**You're in the plot:** Nikeratos, now that he has observed Demeas giving aid to Khrysis, is convinced that Demeas is part of the conspiracy which Khrysis and his own womenfolk have formed. Given what he has seen and heard, he seems rather slow in working out the true state of affairs. Since discovering that his own daughter is the mother, he has dropped the idea – so repugnant to him earlier on – that Moskhion is the child's father.
585	**your son:** at last he realises the truth.
586	**cozened:** lit. 'wrapped me up in fig leaves'. See J. Taillardat, *Les Images d'Aristophane*, Paris[2], p. 134 for the non-metaphorical use of the verb.
588	**walk around:** the imperative form is restored by J. Diggle, *Studies on the Text of Euripides*, Oxford, 1981, 51f. who notes that in dialogue when we have repetition of this kind the second speaker uses the form of the word which the first speaker had used (cf. 303 and Men. *Dysk.* 503 A. let go! B. let go? *aphes! aphes?*).
589f.	Reference to tragedy is common in New Comedy. Our passage has an exact parallel in Men. *Epitr.* 325f. where Syros says to Smikrines 'you've seen tragedy, I know. You must know about Neleus and Pelias'. The effect is not illusion-breaking or illusion-exploiting because tragedy was a

topic any Athenian in real life might raise or discuss (see Bain, 213). There is created, however, a certain piquancy when the junior genre alludes to its theatrical partner. The kind of allusion found here helps put comedy and the plight of the comic characters into a truer perspective. The specific reference here may be to a revival of a play about Danae — Euripidean or Sophoklean — but the story was mentioned in plays which dealt with other topics (cf. Soph. *Ant*.944) and may have become familiar to the fourth-century audience through such a medium.

593 **your roof**: present day readers of the play aware that Plangon was raped on the roof of a house find in this expression a point that escaped readers of C alone. It was, however, on the roof of Demeas' house (40ff.) not Nikeratos' that the incident took place.

594 **gold**: the diminutive form)(*khrysos* (which was used earlier when the reference was to tragedy) is the word for gold in ordinary speech.

596 **you're having me on**: see on 530. Nikeratos realises that all of this is an elaborate joke at his expense.

  as well: as bringing trouble to me and my household.

597 **Akrisios**: Danae's father did not think much of the honour Zeus had done him and his daughter. He cast the daughter and the baby son, Perseus, adrift in the Aegean.

598 How this sentence would have continued had not Nikeratos interrupted is arguable. It seems most likely that the verb in the if-clause means — as it sometimes does in tragedy — 'thought fit to honour' (rather than 'thought fit' sc. to have intercourse with). In this case the missing part of the apodosis would have been 'might he not have similarly honoured *your daughter*'.

599ff. Demeas continues his joke and heightens the farce by referring to two individuals known to the audience who might be 'immortals' (the argument is illogical since unions between gods and mortal women did not always or necessarily produce immortal children). One is the well-known parasite Khairephon who is frequently alluded to by comic poets (he appears also in Matron's parody poem the *Deipnon*, 9 — unfortunately this does not help us to date him). The other person, the totally obscure Androkles, was probably also a parasite (see the introduction, p.xii).

603 **without a contribution**: the *parasite* in comedy (on the origins of the name see W.G. Arnott, *GRBS* 9 [1968] 161ff.) was a sponger who by flattery and by making himself useful to his patrons imposed himself on rich men (like mercenary soldiers or merchants) who gave him free meals. Khairephon, a real-life example of this type, never has to bring a contribution of his own (*symbolē*) to a meal (the allusion is to a type of dinner, *deipnon apo symbolōn*, where each guest brought something of his own or contributed his share in cash).

606-11 These lines are absent from B. It is more likely that this is the result of a copyist's error (the writer's eye leapt from the end of 605 to the similar-looking end of 611) than that 606-11 are an interpolation in C or that B gives us an alternative, abbreviated version of Menander's original script.

606f. The point of these lines (and their punctuation) is obscure, especially regarding the two colour-adjectives. For suggestions see Sandbach ad loc. A reference to Androkles' apparent agelessness would be appropriate since it would constitute proof of his immortality. The gods, as well as living forever, never age.

608 Since *ou* does not normally follow the verb in interrogative sentences one has to assume a change of construction of the kind implied in the translation (for an utterance that starts as statement and changes to question cf. Euboulos fr. 117.7f. — though there hesitation (affected as it happens) is manifest) or else, with Moorhouse (apud Gomme-Sandbach), emend to *estin pou* 'is I suppose a god' (ironically under-stated). If *ou theos* is right here, Demeas is harking back to *ou theos* in 604.

610 **slaughter the victim**: *sphatte*, the supplement adopted here, is not too short for the space. See L. Koenen, *ZPE* 16 (1975) 133n.2.

612   **if he had been taken then:** the punishments to which an adulterer (*moikhos* — see the note on 717) caught in the *act* was liable might be extremely severe. The offended party could do more or less what he liked with the captive. We are meant to think here of various humiliations that might be inflicted on the adulterer such as the singeing off of his body hair or the insertion of pointed vegetables up his rectum. See K.J. Dover on Aristophanes, *Clouds* 1083. Killing the adulterer is hardly in question here, if we believe the speaker of Lysias, 1.32 who seems to suggest that the offended husband could only kill the adulterer if he had *persuaded* his wife to commit the act. But the actual phrasing of the law referred to there is questionable and the likelihood is that the speaker is stretching a point (see A.R.W. Harrison, *The Law at Athens : The Family and Property*, Oxford 1968, 34f.).

ACT FIVE

This act opens with successive monologues: on their similarities (they are both delivered by returning fugitives) and contrasts see Blundell, 42ff.

622   In ordinary language in the fourth century *hamartanō* and its cognates are commonly used euphemistically of blameworthy acts as well as of simple mistakes and errors of judgment: cf. 704. 707 and *exhamartanō* in 646.

623   **the girl**: it is only when Moskhion apostrophizes Plangon in 630 that he names her. Respectable women were not normally named in public by men talking to outsiders in fifth and fourth century Athens. See A.H.Sommerstein, *Quaderni di Storia* 2 (1980) 393 ff.

624   **the oath**: for this see 53. In similar circumstances, Aeschinus in Terence's *Adelphoe* (adapted from Menander, *Adelphoi b*) swore an oath to the girl he had wronged and to her mother that he would not desert her (Ter. *Ad*.333).

628   **Baktria or Karia**: see introduction, p.xii, n.4.

637   **behave so unsympathetically**: Moskhion is less than fair to Demeas. He forgets that it was his own lack of candour with his father that led to the misunderstanding of act four. If he had confessed the truth as soon as Demeas returned, the trouble would have been avoided.

641   We last saw Parmenon in act three when he ran away from Demeas. He returns now expecting a beating and protesting to the audience that he is not to blame for anything that has happened.

646   **Moskhion**: lit. 'the young master' *trophimos* from *trephō*, 'to rear' is the word slaves use of their (original) master's son (= *erilis filius* in Roman Comedy). Probably we are to take the word as passive = 'nursling': see G.P. Shipp, *Antichthon* 11 (1977) 9.

649f.   There is no need with T.B.L. Webster, *Studies in Menander*, Manchester[2],1960,45 to disbelieve this. The idea may have been Khrysis'. cf. E.Keuls, *ZPE*10 (1973) 16.

651   **one of the household**: Khrysis.

658   **cloak and sword**: two basic items for the man who intends to travel abroad selling his services as a soldier: cf. *Pk*. 354f. *spathē* has a long history, being borrowed into Latin and engendering épéé, spada, etc. It had not yet entered Latin when Plautus was adapting Greek plays: he uses *machaera* in contexts like this (see G.P. Shipp, *Glotta* 34 (1955) 149f.).

660   Parmenon's reply suggests that he regards Moskhion as the most unmilitary of men.

664ff.   Moskhion reveals the purpose of his ruse: he wants the pleasure of hearing his father beg him to stay.

667ff.   Moskhion, like most young men in New Comedy, lacks confidence (cf. 92 and 683ff.).

670   The metre changes to trochaic tetrameters for what remains of the play.
Parmenon, unaware of the recent contretemps, has now learned that all is well. He assumes that Moskhion cannot be aware of this and that his present course of action is determined by his ignorance. As Moskhion's question in 673 makes clear, he has not performed the errand upon which Moskhion sent him.

673ff.   The language is high-flown: *the flame of Hephaistos* is a poetic periphrasis for fire. Passages like this and Men. *Dysk*. 946ff. suggest that high-flown language was a traditional feature of descriptions of feasts in comedy (cf. Hunter on Euboulos fr. 75). On the text of C here see H. Riad,*ZPE* 11 (1973) 209. The subject of *enērktai* is 'the basket' (understood): see the note on 222.

678   **rogue**: lit. 'temple robber', a common term of abuse which has lost is original meaning.

682   **bring out some more news to me**: threateningly = 'just you dare . . .'.

83   **gentlemen:** see on 269. This is the first time in the play that Moskhion uses this mode of addressing the audience. It is possible, however, that his opening monologue from which quite a lot is missing had included such an address.

90   **then where is he?:** Demeas' opening words are addressed back into the house, possibly to a slave who has told him that Parmenon has returned and that Moskhion is outside.

93   **I'm off:** Parmenon's presence would detract from the intimacy of the scene that follows, but there is also a technical reason for taking him off now. The actor playing him must change costume and reappear as Nikeratos if there are only three actors available to perform the play (see the introduction, p.xxi). This is undoubtedly the most convenient time to take him off.

98   cf. what Moskhion told us as the play opened, line 8.

03   The sincerity of this apology is marked by the emotive asyndeton of these three verbs, a device liked by Menander: cf. 728f. and fr. 685 K.-T.

05   **my error:** 'when I thought (mistakenly) that you had wronged me, I kept that thought to myself'. R. Merkelbach, *ZPE* 20(1976) 182ff. suggests emending the verb to the second person *ēgnoeis* which would mean 'your misdemeanour' (or rather 'the misdemeanour I thought you had committed').

06   **enemies:** it is taken for granted that in Athens a family as well as having friends will assuredly have enemies: cf. the passages quoted in Dover, *GPM* 180ff. and 474 above.

13   Nikeratos is speaking to his wife.

  bath: the bride has bathed in water specially brought from the Kallirhoe spring or rather from its fountainhouse Enneakrounos (cf. Thuc. 2.15. 3-6) whose site was probably in the city centre: see E.J. Owens, *Journal of Hellenic Studies*, 102 (1982) 222ff. See Ginouvès (cited on 428) 267ff.

  the wedding: what is meant is the feast in the house of the bride's parents which takes place before the groom arrives to take her to his house. See Jacques, xv n. 1 who refers to Gow on Makhon, 11.

17   **adulterer who has been caught:** *moikhos* is used with wider application than our 'adulterer', *moikheia* includes the acts of a man who has had sexual dealings with any of the women-folk of another man's house (see Sandbach on 591). What Nikeratos is saying is incorrect. Moskhion has confessed his 'adultery': he has not been caught in the act. Therefore, he is not liable to the kind of penalties implicitly threatened in this line (for which see 612).

18   **I'll tie you up:** for tying up an adulterer cf. Ter. *Eun.*955.

  and soon: a formula used when making threats. See Johansen and Whittle on Aiskhylos, *Hiketides* 925.

  As in the previous act, violence appears about to erupt on stage. Nikeratos squares up to a defiant Moskhion who raises his sword.

21   **entreaties:** Moskhion's plural *deomenoi* (applicable only to Demeas) provokes Nikeratos who has said nothing to conciliate him.

23   **bring out the bride:** this is addressed to Nikeratos who exits during the next line.

24f.   For a moment Moskhion and Demeas are alone together and Moskhion can comment candidly on the plea made by Demeas in 695ff., an immediate reply having been prevented by the entrance of Nikeratos. His reaction takes the form of a joke. In case his behaviour appears excessively flippant and heartless it should be pointed out that the address *ō pater* is an affectionate one. See the introduction, p.xix.

  moralizing: lit. 'philosophizing'. New Comedy does not have much time for philosophers and in any case when characters are referred to as 'philosophizing' what they have actually uttered tends to be the commonest of commonplaces — see W. Kroll, *Studien zum Verständnis der römischen Literatur* (reprint Darmstadt, 1973) 85 — so that this is a most unfair description of Demeas' admirably candid and direct speech.

726f. The traditional Athenian marriage-formula occurs often in New Comedy. Here, unusually, there is no dowry offered — or rather a postponement in the paying of the dowry till the death of the father. Nikeratos is poor — in the other instances where such formulae occur the fathers are men of means — and in this instance, even if this had not been the case, a self-confessed adulterer could not expect a dowry when he married the woman he had seduced or raped.

728 **god forbid:** *ho mē genoito* 'which may it not come about' is widespread in Greek literature in contexts where it is hoped that evil may be averted (cf. Aiskhylos, *Seven against Thebes* 5), but since clauses like this are common in wills (note e.g. in Aristotle's will 'if something happens to Nikanor (his son-in-law) first — *ho mē genoito*' Diogenes Laertius 5.12, cf. also R. Merkelbach, *ZPE* 19 (1975) 86) it does not seem fanciful to believe that Nikeratos is here jokingly employing legal terminology.

728-9 **I have, I take, I cherish:** see the note on 703f.

729 **bath water:** Plangon has taken the ritual bath, Moskhion has not. See on 713.

730 This is all the recompense, in public at any rate, Khrysis wins for her tribulations during the course of the play. See the introduction, p.xviii.

731 **a torch and garlands:** New Comedy preserves the comastic ending characteristic of Old Comedy. We are made aware through the mention of torches that it is now evening.

732 **deck your head:** the verb belongs to poetic diction and the omission of the article with the body-part is not a feature of spoken Attic.

733 **lovely boys:** the tone is erotic: see K.J. Dover, *Greek Homosexuality*, London, 1978, 15f. It is a moot point whether the absence of mention of 'women' represents a failure to acknowledge the female element in the audience or a reflection of their absence.

733ff. Those plays of New Comedy of which we possess the endings, all display something similar to what is found here, an appeal to the spectators for their applause followed by a formulaic prayer that Victory may attend the players (cf. Men. *Dysk.* 965ff., *Mis.*463ff.). Here we have a version that is expanded and more elaborate: it has to be accommodated to longer lines (the other plays end with trimeters). *prophētēn* and *Bakchiōi* are stylistically elevated. The last three words of 734 coincide with the penultimate line of Antiphanes, *Anthropogonia CGFPR* 3 [2], a play probably produced at least forty years before *Samia*.

737 All dramatic pretence is here abandoned and Demeas speaks for the poet, using language that must derive from a time when the chorus had a more important role in the play than it does in *Samia*.

FRAGMENT

If this fragment has not been erroneously assigned to our play because of its superficial resemblance to line 158, it most likely contains a reference to an offering that is unconnected with the marriage of Moskhion and Plangon, either in thanksgiving for safe return proffered by Demeas (at the end of act one) or to speed up Demeas' return, perhaps the occasion of Khrysis' first entrance (that is to say a passage within the lacuna between 57 and 59). The latter is the suggestion of K. Gaiser, *GB* 5 (1976) 100n.2. Tryphe will be a mute attendant (or else someone who does not appear but is addressed by Khrysis speaking into the house).

WITHDRAWN